QUIET VOICE
FEARLESS LEADER

10 Principles For Introverts To Awaken The Leader Inside

BY TERRANCE LEE, MBA

FRENCHTOWN PUBLISHING

Quiet Voice Fearless Leader

First Edition Published April 2021
Copyright © 2021 by Lee Enterprise Group LLC

ISBN 978-1-7370007-0-9 (ebook)

ISBN 978-1-7370007-1-6 (softcover)

Cover Design by: Safeer Ahmed

Editor: Oluwadamilola Omotuyi

I dedicate this book to my home team:

My son Amari,

My daughter Aminah,

And to my rock, my partner, my best friend...my wife Octavia.
Thank you for believing in me.

CONTENTS

Introduction 1

CHAPTER 1 – VALUE 13

Brothers 15

Introvert Influence. 19

Shonda Rhimes. 19

Warren Buffet 21

J.K. Rowlings 22

Barack Obama. 23

THREE PILLARS OF VALUE 25

Focus on what makes you unique 26

Establish presence 27

Challenge ideas 29

What Introverts Wish Extroverts knew 31

Plan of Action. 32

CHAPTER 2 – COURAGE 35

The Master Asker 39

Introvert turned Party Promoter. 43

THREE PILLARS OF COURAGE 49

Ask the right questions 50

Understand the pros and cons 52

Make a decision and rally the team to believe in it. 54

What Introverts Wish Extroverts knew 56

Plan of Action. 56

CHAPTER 3 – TRUST 59

Mom - The Fighter 61

Boycott 65

THREE PILLARS OF TRUST **69**

Solve Your Team's Biggest Problems 70

The team takes on the personality of its leader 71

Bad News doesn't get better with time 74

What Introverts Wish Extroverts knew 76

Plan of Action 76

CHAPTER 4 – ACCOUNTABILITY **79**

The College "Almost" Graduate 82

Fred Lee Sr. – Quiet Strength 85

THREE PILLARS OF ACCOUNTABILITY **89**

Retrain your mind 90

Always be taking action 92

Never give up 94

What Introverts Wish Extroverts knew 96

Plan of Action 96

CHAPTER 5 – HUMILITY **99**

The absent brother, the absent son 101

THREE PILLARS OF HUMILITY **105**

Celebrate small wins 106

Give your teammates the credit 107

Shield your team 109

What Introverts Wish Extroverts knew 111

Plan of Action 111

CHAPTER 6 – AUTHENTICITY **113**

Dad – The Standard 116

Fake Excited 120

THREE PILLARS OF AUTHENTICITY **124**

Never compare yourself to ANYONE 125

Love Yourself 127

Never compromise your integrity 128

What Introverts Wish Extroverts knew 131

Plan of Action 131

CHAPTER 7 – COLLABORATION **133**

My career was just a phone call away 135

THREE PILLARS OF COLLABORATION **141**

The Power of "I don't know" 142

Who's on your team? 144

The art of delegation 147

What Introverts Wish Extroverts knew 149

Plan of Action 149

CHAPTER 8 – CONFIDENCE **151**

Sink or Swim 153

When Practice Pays Off. 155

THREE PILLARS OF CONFIDENCE **158**

When you get nervous 159

Practice, Practice, Practice 162

What's your mantra? 164

What Introverts Wish Extroverts knew 166

Plan of Action 167

Bonus Section - Delivering Effective Presentations 168

CHAPTER 9 – SERVICE **175**

Tallahassee Roots 178

THREE PILLARS OF SERVICE **183**

Start with your circle of influence. 184

Serve When Nobody is watching 185

Build On Potential 188

What Introverts Wish Extroverts knew 189

Plan of Action 189

CHAPTER 10 – EFFORT **191**

From free college to 10 years of student loan debt 194

Student of the Year 198

THREE PILLARS OF EFFORT **201**

Master your craft 202

Set measurable and attainable goals for yourself 204

Have someone to hold you accountable 206

What Introverts Wish Extroverts knew 208

Plan of Action 209

CONCLUSION **211**

Acknowledgments 215

INTRODUCTION

When I was 13 years old, a choir director said something to me at school one day that damaged my confidence for over 20 years. I grew up as an extremely outgoing, active, and talkative kid. At school and at home, I loved expressing myself through creative writing, basketball, running track, baseball, art, speaking, singing, and playing the piano, among other hobbies. I was usually the kid that was the first to raise my hand when the teacher asked a question in class. When called on, which was often, I would walk to the chalkboard, write out the problem, and explain my answer to the class with authority and confidence. I had a passion for writing, so I had notebooks full of fictional stories with characters that I had created, poems, and songs, until that one day in the seventh grade.

After that day, I stopped raising my hand in class even when I knew the answer; at the lunch table with my friends, I found myself becoming quieter and more reserved. Before that day, I would regularly volunteer to be the leader for team science projects and math competitions. Now I would purposely sit in the back of the class, hoping to never be called on to lead anything. From that point on, it was as if a switch flipped in my mind that I couldn't control. My unwavering confidence, charisma, and self-assuredness quickly became replaced with doubt, fear, and uncertainty. These feelings carried well into my adulthood, invisible weights that seemed to never go away. I'm unsure of what happened to me that day, but from that moment on, I knew something had changed. Read carefully; let me take you on a journey into my past.

PROLOGUE

THE LOSS OF CONFIDENCE

It was a snowy winter day in 1994 in Rochester, New York. At the time, one of my favorite extracurricular activities was being a tenor in the school choir. I was put in the tenor section because I had developed a deeper voice by that time than most of the other kids that were my age. Teachers would tell me all the time that I sounded like I was in high school. Although basketball was my first love and what I was mostly known for, singing and writing music was a close second. My mom was a music teacher and choir director, so I grew up hearing gospel music daily in our house, as well as attending concerts where she would be directing her various school and church choirs. So that definitely had a profound impact on my love for music.

There were about 20 kids in our choir, split evenly between boys and girls of various races and backgrounds. Over a period of a few weeks, I had sensed a growing tension between the choir director and me. I couldn't really tell what it was, but I remember the stern glances she would give in my direction at times when we would be singing. She would regularly stop playing on her piano to direct one of us to correct our notes, but for some reason, her tone with me always came off as more agitated. The nickname that most family, friends, coaches and teachers knew me by at this time was Terry, as opposed to Terrance.

By this point, I had gotten used to the choir director calling me out by my full name in front of everyone, and it normally was not because I had done something right. She would demonstrate how she wanted the notes that I was singing to go, I would then attempt to sing it the way she described. No matter how many times I did, it just never seemed to be good enough.

It also was frustrating to be constantly singled out in front of my peers and friends. It got to the point where I didn't know what to expect each day. Would she be in a bad mood that day or a good one? "I just have to make sure and not mess up" is what I would tell myself, or maybe I can sing a little lower so that she won't be able to hear me.

It all came to a climax one afternoon. She began to play the melody to our first song of the day on the piano. Alongside other members of the choir, I stood up straight on the risers in preparation. The sopranos sang their portion of the song, followed by the alto section. Next up was my section, the tenors, which included 3 other boys and me. I stood there and began to sing my heart out, wanting so badly to impress her. Within a few seconds, she stopped the music and slammed the piano cover down in frustration. The room fell deafly silent; each of us stood there fearfully waiting to see who she was going to call out. She turned her head, starring angrily in my direction, and with a strong tone in front of everyone, yelled,

"Terry Lee, you are off-key! You know what, you need to stop, just stop singing!"

I stood there speechless and in shock. Behind me, I could hear the quiet chuckle from several of my classmates that were standing on the riser above mine, who found humor in my moment of humiliation. With nothing to say, I dropped my head to my chest, unable to move and completely embarrassed. She proceeded to continue playing the piano, and as the rest of the class resumed singing, I stood there quietly. When I got home that night, I took every notebook I had with my stories, poems, and songs that I had been writing since I was 9 years old and threw them all into the trash.

WHO'S THE LEADER IN THE ROOM?

What makes a person a leader versus a follower? What makes a person an extrovert or an introvert? The answers to these questions are complicated and oftentimes are not clear. There is an age-old debate of whether leaders are born or made. Some would say that they could look at a 4 or

5-year-old child and already see the qualities of a future leader. Or perhaps the environment someone grows up in may have an impact on if they'll end up exhibiting leadership qualities. Some would debate and say that a person may not be viewed as having leadership potential in school, for example, but if they are surrounded with the proper tools and training, then they can develop those skills. The topic of personality types is even more complicated. One of the most recognizable personality type tests is the Myers-Briggs Type Indicator. The MBTI approach results in 16 unique personality types that vary from people that are extremely extroverted, to extremely introverted, to falling somewhere in between.

In general, if you have a room of 10 people where 5 people in the room are doing the most talking and exchanging the most information, those 5 will typically be viewed as the leaders in that room. This goes beyond the work or business environment and usually extends into social situations as well. The extrovert loves to interact with other people, and because they talk more, many people naturally view them as someone that would tend to have the "take charge" attitude that most people associate with leadership. Now, what about the other 5 people in that room? A few of them may be offering thoughts here and there but might be overshadowed by the louder voices of the extroverts in the room and spend more time listening. Others may barely be saying anything, which oftentimes gets misinterpreted as them being quiet or disinterested. People in the room rarely ask their opinion on the topic being discussed, and as a result, they end up not contributing to the conversation.

As a whole, if someone were behind a glass wall observing the room of 10 people and their interactions over a one-hour period, they would ultimately draw conclusions about each person. However, it may not always be as clear-cut as you think, and those conclusions might be completely false. What if I told you that one of the five extroverts in the room was actually extremely insecure. As a result, they always express how much they know about every topic in front of others as a form of self-validation.

Also, it could turn out that one of the five introverted or quieter people in the room is actually an extremely accomplished leader who has led teams comprised of hundreds of people. The reason he or she is quiet is that they're listening to the conversations in the room to help gauge the thoughts, talents, strengths, and weaknesses of the people in front of them. These are the type of realities that would be almost impossible for someone to pick up on through brief observation.

One of the goals of this book is to challenge the idea of whom the real leader in the room is. If you're like me, then maybe you never viewed yourself as a leader because you're not typically one of the loudest people in the room. Or maybe your personality is more like one of the 5 extroverts that I described earlier; maybe you've always just assumed that you have things under control and leading comes easy for you. You naturally have more leadership potential than the laid-back co-worker, business partner, family member, or friend you know because they simply don't communicate as much as you do... right? I want to challenge this entire thought process as well. The reality is that extroverts can be great leaders, and introverts can be great leaders as well.

STEREOTYPES & LABELS

Throughout various points of my life toward the end of middle school after the choir incident, transitioning into high school, then college, later in my career, and in various friendships and relationships, I've heard the following words used to describe me: calm, cool, laid back, quiet, relaxed.

Have you ever heard any words like these used to describe you? If so, then people most likely think you're an introvert, and chances are you most likely are one. Over time, we (society) have generally learned to associate the term "introvert" with people that are either socially awkward, shy, insecure, or unsure of themselves. We typically picture them as people that would rather curl up on the couch alone with a good book or sit alone at a local coffee shop enjoying their coffee while avoiding any social interaction. Meanwhile, the extroverts are out conquering the world, making moves in their professional lives, and leading others to greatness. Unfortunately, that is often the perception that many people have. Now the truth is, reading a good book and sitting in a coffee shop by myself are both activities that I do all the time and enjoy. At the same time, I love interacting with my family and friends. In fact, it is something that I look forward to.

However, a key difference between an introvert and an extrovert is that where an extrovert feeds off of the energy of other people and longs for it, introverts are typically completely comfortable being by themselves. What is your story, and how would you describe yourself? How do you think other people in your life would describe you? It's important to think about what has made us into who we are today. I wrote this book for people like me. However, it's also for people who may not share my personality type but find themselves struggling with confidence like I did.

Disclaimer: I'm not a self-proclaimed leadership guru or one of the people on social media who seem to have life completely figured out. I'm also not someone that has been delivering life-changing speeches effortlessly in front of crowds of people since I was in kindergarten. You should know that I have no issue with those people because if you have lived a life free of insecurities and never had issues with confidence, then I truly salute you. But for people who may be dealing with social insecurities, who may hesitate to speak their opinion in a crowd, or who may shy away from opportunities that require them to speak up, I wrote this book with you in mind. You may not realize this, but there are qualities in you that make you perfect for leadership. Has anyone ever told you that? Maybe, but assuming without conceding that no one has, or that someone did, and you doubted that person, know now that it is true; you have traits that the majority of people in this world know nothing about and cannot appreciate simply because they do not understand.

ACTION

I'm big on action over words. Whether someone is discussing what should be done to correct a decline in their company's sales or someone is a part of a social justice movement where they are hoping to impact legislation and change the world. If there is no executable action plan in place, then it's all just words. The purpose of this book is not to just talk about leadership, give some quick tips, and hope that you give it a 5-star rating. My goal is that with each chapter, you will be able to find a few nuggets of truth that you can apply to your life immediately. The concepts that you'll read are not theory. They are based on direct experiences that I've had in my career while leading teams through a variety of high-stress situations with real-life consequences to consider and aggressive deadlines to meet. It is also based on my observations of countless other leaders (good AND bad) in action over my 15-year career in the defense industry as an engineer and in various business ventures that I've been a part of.

Lastly, it is based on several of the mistakes and lessons that I've learned in my personal life and how those experiences have impacted my mindset today as a leader. Each chapter will introduce a key principle that I believe to be critical for leading teams. There are then 3 pillars to focus on as a takeaway from the chapter. I also feel like it is important for people with more extroverted personalities to understand how the mind of an introvert works. On that note, there will be a tip in each chapter for extroverts to learn more about how introverts typically think. Lastly, each chapter will conclude with an executable action plan that is based on each pillar. Again, the goal of this will be all about taking action.

Throughout this book, you'll hear the word "team" used a lot. To clarify, when I'm referring to the leadership of teams, it could apply to a number of different scenarios. It doesn't matter if the team is 3 people or 300. If you're in a position where you are going to be making decisions and executing anything for a group, then you are a leader. Companies have leaders at various levels, entrepreneurs are leaders and typically interact with other leaders, non-profit and volunteer organizations have leaders, a classroom full of students has a teacher as the leader, those same students have leaders in their extracurricular activities and friend groups, families have leaders, communities have leaders...and the list goes on and on. Leadership exists at every level in just about everything that we do. Therefore, when I'm talking about you being the leader of a team that could apply for wherever you are right now and for wherever it is that you're trying to go.

This book is meant to stretch you and even make you uncomfortable at times. To come out of one's comfort zone is something that is scary for most people, not just introverts. Change is always difficult at first, but ultimately if you implement the principles carefully laid down in this book, then my hope is that you'll find yourself starting to evolve into a new person. With that said, I want to be clear that this book's purpose is not to change your introversion because being an introvert is not the problem. We will simply be exploring core ideals that can be adopted and practiced.

THE PAIN, THE PROGRESS

Over the past few years, the thought has crossed my mind to look up the choir director that told me to stop singing that day. I've thought to look her up on social media or to google her name to see if anything would come up. Anytime I have those thoughts, I end up not doing it. It's an incident that I never talked about and kept hidden for years from some of

HERE...

my closest family and friends. For some reason, I've found myself thinking about it more recently, maybe because my son will be leaving daycare and entering school this year. If there is anyone that understands the power that words can have on a person's self-esteem, whether positive or negative, it's me. For a long time the thought of what happened that day made me angry. I wanted to meet her face to face to curse her out, and to tell her about the years of damage that her words caused me to experience. I truly believe that incident was when I began to doubt myself, to question the validity of my words before I would speak to others, and to begin to constantly worry about what other people were thinking about me. But as I've embarked on a spiritual journey over the past several years, working to grow in my faith as a Christian (an area where I have a long way to go), I realized that in order to reach my full potential in life I had to let go of that anger. So, although the situation did affect me severely, it was meant to be a part of my journey.

So, again, I may not be a leadership guru, but I am someone that used to sit along the wall in meetings with my fellow engineers and keep my thoughts to myself. Now I am regularly the one leading meetings where teams are looking to me to provide guidance and direction. I used to literally feel my throat tighten and hands sweat whenever I had to give a presentation, regardless of whether there were 6 people in the room or 60. Now I find myself giving presentations regularly to Vice Presidents and Senior Directors, confident in my subject matter and confident that I can keep control of the room. I used to try to do everything by myself and would avoid collaborating with anybody. Now I work frequently with teams. I often network to create new relationships and focus on building winning cultures within the teams that I lead. I have so far to go and so much more to learn, but I also recognize how far that 13-year old kid that was walking around unsure of himself has come.

It's Your Time

As I stated earlier, I'm nowhere near perfect, and every day, I continue to learn new things, relentlessly striving to be a better version of myself. Professionally, I am currently a section manager for a team of engineers with 20 direct reports on my team and a project manager for a team of over 30 engineers at a Fortune 500 defense contractor. In my personal life, I have my favorite team, where I'm blessed to have my wife Octavia and our two kids Amari (age 5) and Aminah (age 3). Life gets very busy, and honestly, the level of responsibility that comes with knowing there are several people that depend on me can be a lot. At the same time, I wouldn't change it for the world, and I love where I am. I have read some amazing leadership books that have literally changed my life. When I found myself in leadership positions for the first time, the lessons in those books became like a mentor that I could go to at any time for guidance. My hope is that this book will impact someone's life in the same way.

There is a leader inside of you that is dying to get out and present itself to the world. This book is for the student that knows the answer but is afraid to raise their hand in class because they're nervous about how people might look at them. For the person at work that has a great idea to introduce to the team, but every time they start to raise a hand in the meeting to talk about it, something stops them. It is for that person who has a business idea that they're dying to introduce to the world but lacks the confidence to put it out. You're valuable, and you were uniquely created to bring value to this world. There is only one you, and there's only one shot at this life you were blessed with. Whoever you are, I hope this book will help to bring a level of confidence out of you that you never knew you had. You have what it takes to lead, and I look forward to helping you along the journey.

Chapter 1 – Value

"These days, I'd rather speak up and risk being wrong than keep quiet and miss out on adding value to the room."

Every human interaction is an exchange. When you talk to someone, whether it's face to face, over the phone, text, or email, there is an exchange of information and energy taking place. For example, think about the 5 people that you typically talk to the most throughout your week. After those conversations, do you feel happy, inspired, full of purpose? Or do you feel frustrated, uninspired, or even bored? It's natural for us to want to be surrounded by people who are adding value to our lives. This isn't to say that we won't have disagreements or frustrations at times with the people who inspire us. Generally, we like the feeling of being in a room with people where there is a positive exchange of energy and ideas taking place.

One of the misconceptions about introverts is that they do not bring much to a conversation. More often than not, this happens in situations where an introverted person finds themselves conversing with a group of extroverts. The extroverts are speaking at a rapid pace of what seems like a mile a minute, interrupting and cutting each other off while engaging in their version of an enlightening conversation. Meanwhile, the introvert might be sitting there reflecting on what is being said, or they might be waiting for the perfect opportunity to interject in between each point that is made by one of the extroverts. Or oftentimes, the introvert may eventually go into observer mode, where they decide to allow everyone else to dominate the conversation, even though they might have a compelling thought to share. So, it is misleading to assume that just because someone is quieter during a conversation that they don't have something to offer to the discussion.

For example, you have people that are comfortable and extremely communicative around their core group of friends, but if anyone outside of that circle enters the conversation, they might shut down. Sometimes, and this is usually the case with me, it's because they're observing the new dynamic of the group while also observing the new person. In large groups, say 10 or more people, where the introvert knows everyone personally but hasn't interacted with them all together at once, they again might give off the perception of being more reserved in the conversation. Where the misunderstanding comes in is when people assume that the person is just quiet and has nothing to add. This can have negative consequences as the other people in the conversation will typically write off that person as quiet, which leads to them being labeled.

Throughout my life, I can recall being in so many rooms with people where I wasn't saying much at the time, but my mind was racing with a multitude of thoughts and observations. At the start of my engineering career, it was the same way, where I'd be sitting in meetings where I had a thought that would challenge the team's entire approach on a high visibility project. However, my mindset at the time led me to immediately overthink every situation and scenario. Here's an example of a conversation I would typically have with myself:

What will people say after I express this idea?

Is this really even a good idea I have?

If I say this and I'm wrong, then I'm going to look stupid in front of all of these people

You know what, I'll just sit here and stay quiet.

This scenario is more common than most people realize to the point where now when I'm in any room, whether it's at a social gathering, a meeting at the office, or otherwise if there are 15 people there and 3 of those people are not talking, I naturally gravitate to them and wonder what's going through their minds. I'll typically walk toward those people and try to spark up a conversation. My first thought is usually I bet this person is like me! If it's in a meeting setting, then I'll usually be the one to say, "Hey John, what do you think about all of this?". It almost never fails that when I do that, I'm met with an intriguing response from that person.

With all of that said, the typical introvert that may deal with various forms of social anxiety or that might simply choose to shut down socially would benefit from working on this area. It's ok to not be the most talkative in the room at all times and to be caught up in your thoughts. The danger here is the perception that comes with that. As a leader, it is critical that you are adding value to any room that you're in at all times. Essentially, this means being willing to speak up and having the courage to be ok with being wrong sometimes. I can say that on my leadership journey, as I've started to get more comfortable with challenging ideas and asking questions, I have been wrong on several occasions. But guess what, so has everybody else! Nobody knows everything, so asking questions and having challenging conversations are both healthy things to do. These days I'd much rather speak up and risk being wrong than keep quiet and miss out on adding value to the room. As you grow in your verbal confidence, people will take notice, and the most important part is that you'll start to appreciate your value more as well.

BROTHERS

When I arrived at Florida A&M University in the fall of 1999, I met people that started out as my friends, and eventually became my brothers. There was a group of us that met early on during my freshman year, our primary bond initially was the fact that each of us was from Texas. I stayed on the first floor of Gibbs Hall dormitory on campus, and right across the hall from me were two guys that ended up becoming life long friends of mine, Dave and Harold. Along with them, our group included Keith (KB), O' Neal (Fro), Aaron, James D, Sy, Ant, Dave L and others. People on campus began to refer to us as 'The Texas Boys' anytime we would come around, we literally were always together. A few years later, when Harold, Ant, KB and Fro moved to an apartment complex in Tallahassee called the Orchards, our circle began to grow larger. Our friend group grew to include people like Mendel from Chicago, Charles from Atlanta, Todd (T. Fin) from Ohio and a number of people from all across the country. In addition, in the spring of 2003, I was initiated into Kappa Alpha Psi Fraternity during my junior year. It was a special time, and it truly changed my life forever. The men in my fraternity were people of power and influence on my school's campus and throughout the country. Within our chapter and on my line alone, we had Student Government Association presidents, Mr. Florida A&M, the King of Orange and Green, scholars with 3.9-4.0 grade point averages, and the list goes on.

My grades were ok at the time, my worst semester was now behind me (the spring of my freshman year, which I'll talk about in a later chapter), and I was now starting to get into the core of my electrical engineering major. But it's not like I was at the top of my engineering class. I wasn't involved in any student political organizations or many organizations at all, for that matter. I was a member of the Texas Club, made of students that were attending FAMU from various cities in Texas. We had several events throughout the year and made some amazing memories together, but even with that, I didn't hold any leadership position at the time. Leaving you to ask, what was I doing among this group of dynamic leaders and influencers?

Looking back now, I know that one of the reasons I was blessed to be a part of this fraternity, besides the life-long friendships that I made, was to expose me to leadership. See, I grew up moving around a lot, a total of five times living in five different cities. So, I got used to being in new situations and being uncomfortable around new people. I've noticed that when most kids enter a new environment for the first time, they typically react in one ~~out~~ of two ways:

1) Become the loudest, most boisterous kid in the class. The goal is to gain attention and to get the much-needed acceptance that they desperately want. Since they don't know how long they'll even be around before the next move, they seek to gain as many new friends and become as popular as possible during that time.

2) The second kid takes a different approach...isolation. Instead of seeking attention, this kid prefers to mostly keep to themselves, and if they make new friends, it's usually because that friend approached them. As this kind of child sees it, there's really no need to approach new people and seek out new friendships because they don't know how long they'll be around.

My approach was always the latter. Regardless of that, I always made friends anytime that we moved, typically because I would be adopted as a friend by a group of extroverts when I arrived at the new school. I played basketball, and from the ages of 8 to about 14, I was very tall for my age. That alone got me attention when I would get to a new school. Besides being a basketball player, I was also used to getting ~~get~~ good grades ~~too.~~ Anything less than an A wasn't something I was used to, although that wasn't exactly the way to gain popularity at the time.

Anyway, I bring up specific points from my childhood for context. When I got to FAMU, I was surrounded by people who understood and thought like me. After going through a childhood of moving around and being the awkward new kid in class time and time again, the FAMU experience was what I desperately needed. To then later become a member of such an illustrious fraternity and be surrounded with intelligent, thoughtful, and talented young men was also a feeling of gratification that I can't explain. We understood each other's struggles, triumphs, goals, and dreams. We were all from varying backgrounds and different parts of the country, but there was mutual respect and honor between all of us. When my fraternity brothers spoke, they did so with passion, authority, and confidence. The conversations we would have were about various topics ranging from politics to sports, to entertainment, to finance, and basically anything else that might be the topic of the day.

Similarly, I had the same dynamic with my friends when I would be hanging out at the Orchards. In between watching hours of football together and drinking beers, we would have deep discussions, passionate debates, and express our opinions about life. I would stop by with the intention of staying for a few hours to watch one game, and end up spending my entire weekend there at times. For the first time in my life, it felt cool to be smart; it was cool to talk about your goals because we all were trying to get somewhere. I also got to see young men that were speaking in front of large rooms of people and were completely comfortable doing it. I got to see men that exhibited true leadership during great times and when times were difficult. They say that iron sharpens iron, and that's exactly what being around my friends and my fraternity brothers was doing for me.

These days things are very different from when we were in college. Several of us have families, a few of us have some grey hairs (me being one of them), and we've all evolved as men. Every one of my college friends and fraternity brothers is very different in their own way, and each one of them brings a unique value to any room that they walk into. Although we don't talk and hang out every day like we did in school when we do meet up for a trip, one of them comes through the Dallas area to visit, or we talk on the phone; it's like no time has passed. These days I know what value I bring to the table in any situation, and if I don't know how I will bring value, then I will figure out how. I'm thankful that a kid like me ~~that~~ WHO lacked confidence in so many ways was able to learn from, grow and build with a special group of leaders like I was.

Truthfully, this portion of the book was very hard for me, as one of my best friends and a beloved member of the Texas Boys crew from my freshman year recently passed away as of the date of this writing. Keith Braithwaite (KB) was one of the few people on this planet that understood me. Very few people understand the personality, the quirks and the perspective of an introvert...and Keith was one of the few that did. He was extremely funny, loyal and charismatic; but also carried himself at times with a quiet confidence that ~~me and him~~ he & I understood. I dedicate the remainder of this chapter to him and to his memory, if there's anyone that would have supported a book that was meant to help people, I know he would have. Rest in peace KB, love you forever, bro.

INTROVERT INFLUENCE

Throughout the process of writing this book, I spent a lot of time researching a number of successful introverts. Some were people that I expected to have an introverted personality, while with others, I was completely shocked. Let's explore a few and consider the value that each of them adds to any situation.

SHONDA RHIMES

Television producer, screenwriter and author Shonda Rhimes has become a household name. Her production company, Shondaland, is the force behind successful shows such as Grey's Anatomy, Scandal, How to Get Away with Murder and several others. To give an idea of her longevity and consistency as a creator, the show Grey's Anatomy has been airing on ABC for 17 seasons; a length of time that is almost unheard of in the entertainment industry. Netflix signed Shonda to a deal worth over $100 million to create content for their platform, and she hasn't disappointed. The show Bridgerton has become one of their top series, among others that she has created. Someone with Shonda's level of power and influence in Hollywood would typically be assumed to be a larger than life personality and the life of the party.

However, in interviews, Shonda has mentioned that she has always been introverted. In fact, she got the reputation for consistently declining invitations to social events, preferring to stay at home alone. Her book "The Year of Yes" is her account of a year where she decided to say yes to events and things that she would have normally said no to. Being someone that has avoided social interactions myself at times, I could completely identify with her. Shonda is a force in Hollywood and doesn't appear to be slowing down anytime soon.

Shonda's Value – To create compelling storylines that will capture an audience's attention and have them binge watching for hours, it takes a different kind of mind. The fact that her company Shondaland has so many shows with a number of seasons, means that Shonda's mind is constantly thinking about and creating new characters, plot twists, surprise endings and everything else that comes with a hit show. The value that Shonda brings to the table is clear; exceptional creativity, consistency and the ability to produce high quality content. Networks like ABC and streaming platforms like Netflix have clearly realized Shonda's unique value, because her run has been unlike anything seen in entertainment history. So in the entertainment business where flash and flamboyance seem to dominate the field, Shonda has created her own lane and dominated as an introvert.

WARREN BUFFET

In my mid-twenties, I started to get interested in learning more about the stock market. At that point, the only thing I knew was that I was invested in my company's 401k retirement plan, and every paycheck, a percentage of my earnings would go into it. If someone had asked me what companies I was invested in, how many shares I owned, and what my portfolio mix was, I would have had no idea. I decided to look into books that taught the fundamentals of stock investing, and the one that grabbed my attention was a book written by Robert Hagstrom about the legendary stock investor Warren Buffet titled "The Warren Buffet Way". I was well aware of who Warren Buffet was, as is most of the world. For those that aren't aware, Warren has amassed a fortune of well over $80 Billion dollars as a stock investor.

The perception that I'd always had of Warren was a man in charge with a booming voice and boastful presence. In reality, I found out that when Warren tried to start his first investment group in his early twenties, he was afraid to pitch his idea to other people. This was because of an intense fear that he had of public speaking and presenting to others. Despite this, Warren continued to practice and improve on his speaking abilities. Fast-forward to now, and the majority of people watching Warren talk during interviews (including myself) would have never guessed that inside of him is an introverted personality. Although he is chairman and CEO of the wildly successful investment firm Berkshire Hathaway, which at the time of this writing is trading for over $300,000 per share, Warren still lives in his original home that was built in the 1950s in Nebraska. This, of course, is quite contrary to the lavish multi-million dollar mansion that you would expect a billionaire to have. From watching hours of interviews, it is clear that Warren prefers a simple life, classic introvert behavior.

Warren's Value – One of Warren Buffet's famous phrases states to be "greedy when others are fearful, and be fearful when others are greedy."

This simple philosophy, among the countless other guides of wisdom that have made Warren one of the richest people in the world, speaks to the value he is able to bring to others. Let's face it, there have been millions of people that have invested in the stock market throughout history, but the large majority have never seen a return anywhere close to Buffett's. So naturally, when someone like him is giving advice about investing, you would tend to listen. Ultimately his value is the ability to go in the complete opposite direction of everyone else and to be comfortable when doing so.

J.K. ROWLINGS

The next person is one that I've become fascinated with, merely from the fact that she took a concept in her head and evolved it into a worldwide phenomenon. J.K. Rowlings is the creator of the Harry Potter series, a series that caught fire and became record-breaking. Harry Potter books have sold over 500 million copies worldwide, making it the best-selling book series of all time. The book series eventually became a movie series as well, grossing well over $1 billion dollars in revenue.

Despite all of the success of the Harry Potter franchise, the creator's personality and temperament are not quite what you would expect from someone with a net worth that is estimated to be between $650 million and a billion dollars. In an interview with Elle magazine, J.K. credited her success to being an extreme introvert. In the article, she stated that when the idea for Harry Potter came into her head, she didn't have a pen that worked and was too shy to ask anybody else if she could borrow one. She goes on to say that she believes this was a good thing, as she then sat and thought for several hours conceptualizing the Harry Potter story. Well, eventually, she got a pen, and the rest is history.

J.K's Value – J.K. is a testament to the fact that introverts can be extremely deep thinkers. I'm sure that when the idea for Harry Potter began to form in J.K.'s head, it was an exhilarating feeling, but not a feeling that she would have described to anyone else. Publishers are often looking for the next book that will become an instant classic and a consistent seller, while movie production companies are looking for the next opportunity to release a blockbuster film. But ultimately, in this scenario, the power lies with the creator, and that's where someone like J.K. comes in. Her value is in the fact that her mind can create characters, plots, and situations in her head that will leave a reader and an audience clinging for more. Not bad for someone that was afraid to ask for a pen.

BARACK OBAMA

The 44th president of the United States, Barack Obama, has always been an interesting case study to me in the dynamic of introversion and extroversion. From his own admission, former president Obama is an introvert. In a New York Times article, he stated that his most productive work is done alone in silence, and his closest aides attested to the fact that every night after dinner with his family, Barack would spend several hours in a room working by himself. If you've ever seen Barack speak in front of a crowd, there is no denying the power that he commands on a stage and the ease with which he is able to draw emotion out of the people listening. The level of confidence and poise that Barack exhibited while operating in the most powerful position in the world for 8 years would typically be expected from an extrovert.

Regardless of if you agreed with his politics while in office or agree with his views on various topics now, very few people would disagree that Barack Obama is clearly a leader. From his time as a community organizer in Chicago to his state Senate position and finally becoming the country's first African American president, Barack has been in positions where he has led people. Interestingly enough, from the first time I saw Barack speak to the final address he gave prior to leaving the White House as president for the last time, I knew there was something different about him. He never struck me as the boisterous, loud, narcissistic, or elitist type that many people associate with being the leader of the free world. I couldn't quite figure it out, but when I read the article where Barack explained his working process, it suddenly became completely clear to me.

Barack's Value – I believe that one of the core values that Barack Obama brings to the table in any situation he's involved in is simple, that value is calmness. Reporters, congress members, and others would regularly tee up situations where the majority of people in this world (including many introverts) would have lost their temper. That loss of temper would have resulted in a shouting match or even a physical altercation. No matter how difficult the question, and no matter how disrespectful the accusations or lies are about him, Barack just never seems to get flustered. Truthfully this has at times become a paradox with him and his legacy, as many people (in particular in the African American community) urged Barack to be more assertive, and some have gone as far as to call his demeanor too soft and too weak. Again I'm not here to agree or disagree about what he did while in office, as I don't consider myself to be a political expert by any means. However, I do know calm and cool when I see it. And there is value in being the one person in the room that maintains a level head, remains calm, and can make calculated decisions with confidence.

Beyond the obvious success that each one of them has experienced, what truly separates Shonda, Warren, J.K. and Barack is their value. Value is something that cannot be faked, and each person on this planet has the capacity to add value at some level. What value can you bring to the world? This is an important question; keep that thought in your head as you're reading through the remainder of this chapter.

THREE PILLARS OF VALUE

FOCUS ON WHAT MAKES YOU UNIQUE

Five years into my first engineering job, I was selected for the Engineering Leadership Development Program (ELDP) at my company. It was a program where you got the opportunity to rotate into different job roles across the organization. It was a very selective program, and honestly, I was surprised when I was picked. At the time, I had a certain view of what a leader was, and I certainly didn't fit into that category. Granted, I was a hard worker, and I'd done several important presentations by that point in my career on key projects. But I hadn't led anybody, and I wasn't very engaging in discussions when we had meetings. So, who would've possibly picked me for this program? What I learned after talking to my manager at the time, Roland Williams, was that there were people on the team who had seen leadership potential in me. I remember him telling me and me sitting there nodding my head. But internally, I was thinking to myself, "Who are they talking about? Do they have the right person?".

Regardless, I started the program, and it was life-changing. I got to see different areas of the company, which exposed me to various team dynamics and different styles of leadership. We also had leadership conferences at least once a year, where I learned critical skills like how to run a meeting, tips for public speaking, team building, and countless other topics. Between the leadership program and the fast-paced work environment that I started to be exposed to, it became clear to me that I had a unique skill that everyone else might not have. It's a skill that I'd actually been criticized for at different points in my life, as it can sometimes be misinterpreted for being a lack of passion. However, it has now helped carry me through several extremely high-pressure situations in my career, when deadlines were tight, and failure was not an option. In line with the value noted about former president Obama earlier, my skill is remaining calm under pressure. It takes a lot to get me rattled off of my game. Now, do I get nervous sometimes before a big presentation? Do I feel pressure when

I look at my to-do list that's a mile long, and every task is due today? Of course, I do. However most people around me would never know. Ultimately, I don't let it get to me; I won't allow the pressure to win. It's funny that one of my biggest criticisms from others and criticisms that I had about myself has turned out to be a strength.

What's unique about you? I guarantee there is something that sets you apart from others. It could be a skill that you have, experiences that you've gone through, your ability to analyze difficult problems, your personality or demeanor. Whatever that thing is, I would encourage you to lean into it and to explore it. Be careful to not get caught up in what everyone else is doing. Human nature is that we naturally compare ourselves to other people and assess ourselves against them. This is not only unproductive but is also a quick road to unhappiness. The only standard we should worry about chasing and maintaining is our own because we'll never measure up to anything else. Later in the book, we'll go into more depth with one of the pillars titled 'Never compare yourself to ANYONE.' Other people were made to be who they are, and you were made to be who you are. So your objective is not to live up to the standard of anyone else; it's to discover your unique skill and to cultivate it. High-performing teams operate well when everyone is focusing on their strength. Where one person is weak, there will be another teammate that's strong in that area; this creates a culture where everyone is free to be themselves and to do their best work. So, your uniqueness is something that should be recognized and celebrated; use it to your advantage.

ESTABLISH PRESENCE

If you're in a meeting and you don't say anything, then do you feel like you've added value to the meeting? Now, of course, there are times when your sole purpose for being in a room is to listen, to get an update on recent developments within the team, or a number of other reasons. The issue comes when you become known as the quiet person in the room that never has anything to add to the conversation. Part of adding value to any situation is being able to bring something to the table that is beneficial to others. Think about it like this... what is one major goal that you would love to accomplish in the next 3-5 years? If you were going to pick 5 people that you could get on a conference call right now to discuss and strategize with on that goal, who would those people be? It's most likely people who will offer an opinion on your project, will offer constructive criticism, and will challenge you. If one of the 5 people were on the call and literally didn't say a word, then you'd feel like they weren't needed.

Of course, some of us introverts are used to not being the most talkative person in many group situations. And this isn't to say that if you have a more reserved personality, you need to go out of your way to say something every few minutes just to make sure you're talking. When you do that, you run the risk of it coming off as superficial and fake. Trust me, I've done this, and it doesn't even feel right. If there's nothing to say, then there's just nothing to say. The point is to make your presence felt, to make people recognize that you're a part of the conversation. When you're called on to offer an opinion or input, then you give a direct response; if you have something to interject into the conversation, then you do it. So you might be thinking, "Ok Terrance, easy for you to say. Anytime I get ready to speak up during a conversation like that I become a nervous wreck and I feel uncomfortable." Hey, I understand, I've been there. This pillar of establishing presence might take some time to get used to, and that's perfectly ok. The point is to acknowledge it, and to address it.

So, here's the thing, some people love to hear themselves talk and are going to talk without any prior thought about what's about to come out of their mouth.

Having presence does not mean always being the one to talk; it does not mean you must lead the conversation every time, and it does not mean that you have to be the loudest voice in the room. This is a big misconception, and I know it because I've now observed and worked with enough leaders with varying personalities to see what works and what doesn't. People go into many conversations with the sole purpose for others to hear them, not to hear others. That's not a presence to me, and it's not admirable.

Now you ask, what is presence? Your presence just means that you need to be present at the moment, whatever that moment is. Depending on the situation, presence might mean that you need to sit back and listen for a few minutes to gain a true understanding of the subject matter being discussed before giving a response. There is a phrase that says, 'Better to be quiet and considered a fool, then to open your mouth and remove all doubt.' This often happens when people jump the gun and start talking about topics with no knowledge of what they're talking about. Other times presence might mean that you'll have to speak up more. If you're used to being the quiet one in your circle of friends, co-workers or business associates, then you will need to look to make a conscious effort to seek opportunities to give your input when people are talking. The truth is, your thoughts matter, and your opinion matters, so when given the opportunity, don't be afraid to get it out.

CHALLENGE IDEAS

Conflict, confrontation, push back... some people hate it, while others actually live for it. One of the most boring rooms to me is the room where everyone is always in agreement. When everyone thinks the same way and agrees on every topic, then there's really nothing being said that's pushing anyone to grow. In this scenario, everybody remains in their bubble of thoughts and beliefs. In a team full of different personalities, whether at work, in business, in the family, or otherwise, there are absolutely going to be disagreements. We are human beings with different backgrounds, different belief systems, and different thoughts. And this is perfectly fine. Humans were made to be different, every single one of us. With that said, the key is to embrace people for their differences and be willing to challenge each other. An effective leader is willing to listen to the opinions of others but is also willing to push back or disagree with those opinions. Here's a scenario:

Two co-workers are sitting in a meeting next to each other. There is a conversation happening during the meeting between other people in the room, and points are being made that neither of them agrees with. The meeting continues with the two co-workers not saying anything, just exchanging an occasional look between each other that signals 'These people have no idea what they're talking about." After the meeting concludes, they both go around the corner to the break room and start talking about how stupid the idea they just heard in that meeting was. They exchange a number of reasons why it was stupid and what they would have done or said differently.

Does this sound like anybody you know or has this been you before? Let's rewind time back to this meeting. When the two co-workers were sitting there, and they heard the comment made that they disagreed with, let's assume one of them spoke up and said, "Actually, I think we should consider a different approach." The people in the room turn in their seats to look in that person's direction, and that person then proceeds to share their thoughts in the meeting instead of voicing them to their co-worker in the break room. Now one of two things will happen. Firstly, what was just said is going to spark a conversation, and ideas about it are going to start being exchanged. That conversation may now lead to support for the new approach as an alternative. Hence that person has now officially brought value to the room. The other outcome is that they share their thoughts and have partial agreement from others in the room, or they receive complete disagreement from everyone. Either way, people may not say it, but they will respect that person more because they had the courage to speak up, and especially the courage to disagree.

I realize this is not an easy thing for some people, and this is not specific to introverts as I have encountered a number of extroverts that avoid conflict as well. A lot of people prefer to keep peace and avoid any problems; in theory, it sounds like it's the easier way to live life. But a leader can't operate this way. A leader has to speak up when something is being done that doesn't line up with the mission of the team. A leader also has to be willing to accept varying thoughts from others that might disagree with their own. Having an exceptional team means being surrounded by people that might disagree with and challenge you. When your team faces hard times and your plan has been altered (which will inevitably happen), you want people around that don't all process information the same way that you do. Build a culture that encourages each other to challenge ideas and to respectfully disagree, because nobody grows from being in a boring room.

WHAT INTROVERTS WISH EXTROVERTS KNEW

When we're all in a room or on a call together, it might seem like I'm quiet. But the truth is, I have a lot to say and have a ton of ideas. My ideas can bring significant value to the ongoing conversation, but I might hesitate at times to speak up, oftentimes because I am processing and thinking about what is being said. Where you are quick to talk, I might not be depending on the situation. For me to feel comfortable sharing my thoughts with the team, I work best in an environment that feels open and is free of judgement. It's also difficult to add value when everyone else is constantly talking, and I'm trying to figure out where to fit my words in. When I know that you care about my opinion, when you create a space where I feel like I will be heard, and when you allow me to be myself then I can begin to open up to you and provide value to the team.

Plan of Action

Focus on what makes you unique - Write down one or more unique qualities that make you different from other people that you interact with regularly. It doesn't have to be something monumental; if you think it's something that is small, then I still want you to write it down. After writing it down, I want you to think about how your unique skill could be used to benefit others. Keep that list with you or put it up on a wall where you can see it every day, and start to look for ways to utilize that skill in your daily interactions with people.

Establish Presence – If you have an important group meeting or discussion that is coming up at work, at your business, at a place that you volunteer, in your family, or anywhere - I want you to write down one thought that you have that could contribute to the conversation and help solve a problem that the group is currently experiencing. Then I want you to have the courage to bring that thought up during the next conversation. Don't worry about what people will think about you or if they'll judge you. Guess what, you're not perfect, and they're not either! You have a thought that needs to get out to the world, so get it out.

Challenge Ideas - What is an idea that the team you're on believes in that you think could be changed for the better? Write that idea down (and now the hard part...), in your next team meeting or discussion, bring up the following:

- o Why you don't agree with the idea
- o The idea or solution you believe it should be replaced with
- o Actionable steps for how the team can implement the new idea

The key to this step (this is VERY important) is to not disagree with something unless you have a solution to fix it. That's why it is critical to think through the 3 steps above before doing this. Once you've established a plan, then it's time to go for it and let your voice be heard.

By the way, I thought it might be helpful to provide a resource for you that can be used as you're reading this book. I've created a free worksheet that is available for you to download. This worksheet includes all of the book's leadership pillars from each chapter, and space for you to take notes on the action plans. To download the worksheet you can go to www.quietvoice-fearlessleader.com/freeresources.

CHAPTER 2 – COURAGE

"When your team sees how bold and how confident you are in your decision making, then they will naturally believe in the mission and believe in you."

In our society, everybody wants to be seen and wants to be heard. Reality television, where the highest-rated shows oftentimes have people screaming at each other and occasionally throwing a drink at the other person, is one example. It seems like the person who is the loudest, and the most obnoxious is usually seen as interesting, and as a result, might end up with a spin-off show or company endorsement deals. Or the political debate shows on CNN, Fox News, CNBC, or other news networks where a political liberal and conservative are shown on a split-screen with a moderator in the middle. They go back and forth on whatever the topic of the day is, interrupting and cutting each other off and preparing a response before the other person is anywhere near done speaking.

How about in our relationships with our significant others and our family members? If we're honest, whenever we're in the middle of a heated disagreement, how many of us actually listen to every single word the other person is saying and digest what was said before we say something back? If this is you, then you'll get no judgment from me because I share the same struggle. Leading to the question, what makes listening so hard? Maybe a better question is why is the quality of being a good listener not celebrated?

For me, the picture of a leader that I had in my head for years was the person that walks into a room of 20 people, and says:

"Alright team... our current forecast is showing that our delivery date is on track to be 3 months late to the customer. But here's what we're about to do."

The leader then spends the next 30 minutes directing each person on the team and assigning tasks; they speak loudly and with extreme confidence. They don't ask many questions because they already have all the answers. To ask questions would appear weak, and besides, they are the leader, so they run the room. During the 30-minute meeting, everyone in the room is watching the leader, impressed by their "take charge" attitude. At the conclusion of the 30 minutes, the leader asks,

"Ok, team, we're ready to go; any questions?"

The room is typically silent. Everyone has their marching orders and knows what needs to be done, so no need for questions. If a question is asked, then the leader usually gives a quick, pointed response. If the question is one that challenges the leader's approach in any way, then it is met with swift resistance and shut down immediately:

"Well, that's just something we'll have to worry about later. That's irrelevant to what needs to be done today."

The person who asked the challenging question will most likely not dare to ask again in the future and leaves the room thinking how stupid they were to speak up at that moment. This is what I pictured in my mind in the past whenever I would hear the word 'leader,' and I can say that as my career has progressed in the defense industry, I have run into this leadership style at several points and have seen the outcome of it.

Now let's take the same scenario of a room with 20 people, but with a different leader. The leader walks into the room and says:

"Alright, team, here's the situation; our current forecast is showing that our delivery date is on track to be 3 months late to the customer. Now I have some ideas that could help us to mitigate the current issues that we have and pull in our schedule, but I want to hear from everyone. So let's discuss."

The next 30 minutes are spent with everyone in the room exchanging ideas for how to pull the schedule in. The leader didn't know this, but from discussions, it turns out that 3 people in the room have contacts in the department that is currently producing the product. They take action during the meeting to work with that department on getting the product moved up in priority. There are also several people that bring up parallel paths that can be worked at the same time in the event that the original plan just isn't going to work. These are parallel paths that the leader had never considered and didn't even know were possible. The meeting concludes with everyone in the room feeling like something was accomplished, and a once dire 3-month schedule slip now has the potential to be mitigated, which could lead to an on-time delivery to the customer.

Which type of leaders have you encountered in your life, and which personality type are you? The example above is in a work environment, but it applies to almost any situation where group interaction is involved. There are people that would say the take-charge approach of the first leader is the way to get things done. Formulate a plan, then drive the team to believe in it. Then there are people who prefer the approach of the second leader, where the focus is more geared toward collaboration and a collective answer to the problem. So which approach is right?

If your personality is more introverted, do you have to learn how to become the person that bursts into the room pointing out directions and giving assignments without anyone's input? The conclusion I've ultimately drawn is that there is nothing empowering, inspiring, or productive to a team about having a leader that is unwilling to listen. Teams that operate under this leadership style quickly turn into a dictatorship, as opposed to a democracy. I'll propose to you that one of the most critical traits of a good leader is the ability to make decisions, and this can rarely be done alone in a vacuum. Most people naturally want to be led. They don't necessarily want to lead, and as a leader, I find myself constantly making decisions; some of those decisions might be small while others can be

QUIET VOICE FEARLESS LEADER

extremely difficult and complicated. If you want to grow into a leader, then it is imperative that you become a decision-maker. Now, this can be difficult for some introverts to do, which is why I learned an approach that has been a huge help for me. It is definitely not something that is mastered overnight, but the best leaders that I've observed and worked with always do this. To make good decisions, you must do the following in this order:

1. Ask Questions and Listen

2. Understand the Pros and Cons of each decision path

3. Make a Decision and Rally the Team behind it

That's it. If you have a decision to make, ask questions, then listen to the answers given. From those answers, confirm your understanding of what was said, then make your decision. Do this over and over again just to get practice. It doesn't have to be a major decision in your career or your business. It can be something small, a conversation about where to eat dinner with your wife or husband, for example. Which by the way, is a huge deal in my home; for example, my wife is what you would call a foodie, so I can name 30 restaurants for us to try for dinner, and she'll say no to every single one. What we're going to eat for dinner quickly becomes a serious decision with us! You probably get the point. Start to apply this and watch how it will change your approach to decisions forever. The reality is that most people make decisions in this order:

1. Ask

2. Pretend to Listen

3. Assume They Understand

4. Make a Decision

If you want to be like the majority of people in the world, take the above approach. But I know that's not what you want, and that's not why you're reading this book. You're reading this because you want to grow, and you want to be different. In order to do that, you'll have to learn to become a master decision-maker.

THE MASTER ASKER

I started my first entrepreneurial endeavor in the summer of 2007. At the time, I was introduced to a multi-level marketing company, which I joined with hopes of adding an additional income stream to go along with my engineering job. This was right around the time that I was introduced to the book 'Rich Dad, Poor Dad' written by Robert Kiyosaki. Up to that point, everything that I'd learned about money was that I needed to excel in school, get a solid career coming out of college, work for 40 years and retire. Like many others, that book completely changed my perspective on money and my approach to it. As soon as I finished reading that book, I was eager to start a business and was open to the first opportunity that was available. At the time, my ex-girlfriend had just joined the company, so she introduced me to it, and I signed up. For those unfamiliar with network marketing, the structure of most companies is typically that income is made two primary ways: through the sale of products and through recruiting new members into the business. At some point, you may have heard of businesses like this referred to as pyramid schemes and talked about in a negative way. I will say this, as someone that was a part of 4 different multi-level marketing companies over a 6-year period, I have nothing bad to say about my experiences and wouldn't discourage anyone from getting involved in one if they feel the opportunity is right for them. In fact, through that first business, I was able to meet someone that gave me a new perspective on life while also introducing me to leadership concepts that I still use today.

Our team's up line leader and sponsor was a man named Cedrick Harris. He was an amazing communicator, full of energy, and clearly a leader. He was also the first millionaire that I'd ever met in my life and the first person I'd met that didn't work for someone else. I was only a part of his team for 3 months, but despite my time in the business being short, I learned several lessons. One of the critical lessons that I learned from Cedrick was the importance of listening to people before speaking. In multi-level marketing, or in any sales transaction, you have a good or service that you're looking to sell to someone. In that business, either you were selling them on the idea of how your product could add value to them or selling the idea of how being a part of the business could add value to them.

One of the first things I was asked to do was to write a list of everyone that I knew, friends, family, co-workers, etc., and their phone numbers. From there, the system was supposed to be that you reached out and asked that person if they were interested in having an additional income stream or if they were interested in saving money on products that they were already using. Once that person said they were interested, then you were supposed to tell them you would schedule a 3-way call with your up-line leader so they could hear more about the opportunity. Now it was very common for people to ask things like, "Well, tell me, first what is it?" Something that newbies like myself at the time would typically do is then try to explain the entire business that we'd just joined. About 90% of the time, this would end up with me fumbling over words for 30 minutes on the phone with my friend or family member trying to explain the business and how great it would be for them, which they would then respond with, "That's cool man, yeah I'm gonna think about it." We would get off of the phone, and I wouldn't hear from them at all. If I called or texted to follow up and said, "Hey, what's up, so what are your thoughts on what we talked about?" it would either be no response or a quick "Yeah I haven't really got to it yet" or "I'm actually not interested, hope it works for you though."

The truth is from the time I opened my mouth on the first phone call, I was over-eager, and I was anxious to get my first business partner so that I could get a bonus payment from the company. And I'm sure it was obvious to anyone on the other end of the phone with me. I was not speaking from a position of strength but from a position of desperation, and people can pick up on that. Now here's how the system was supposed to work...

After running through over half of my call list with no success, I was reminded by other business partners that I was supposed to be following the system and doing 3 way calls with my upline leaders. I was one of those guys that prided myself on being self-sufficient. Give me the bare necessities, and I'll figure out a way to make something work. Well, it was time to swallow that pride and accept some help. I'll never forget my first few 3-way calls where it was me, Cedrick, and one of my friends on the phone. The format was to introduce my friend to Cedrick, taking time to edify him, so the person on the line was made aware of his resume and accomplishments in the business. From there, I would put the phone on mute and let Cedrick have a discussion with them.

What I remember the most about those calls was that they were the complete opposite of what I expected. I'd expected that as soon as I introduced him, he would start talking a mile a minute, breaking down every product in the company's portfolio and details about every last dollar that could be made by the person that was listening. To my surprise, he spent the first 5 to 10 minutes of the phone call asking the person questions. I remember the first call when he was doing it, sitting there thinking, "Dude... we're supposed to be selling; why are you asking all these questions?" I just didn't understand at the time. What I didn't know was that what he was doing was a basic skill that anyone that ever wants to lead or influence people should learn.

You see, we're constantly selling every day. If you and your co-workers are in a meeting and two people disagree about something, in that exchange, each of them is trying to sell the other person on their thought process.

When people have disagreements with their significant other oftentimes their desire is to be heard. They're trying to sell the other person on their viewpoint, in an attempt to be understood. Selling is happening all around us, but most of the time, it's not done well. The reason that Cedrick was asking questions and listening intently to each person's answers is that he wanted to learn about who he was talking to. For example, someone like me is very analytical and structured. If someone wants to get my attention, they're not going to impress me by talking about luxury cars or vacations that I can have if I join their business venture. However, if they show me the numbers, and the numbers make sense to me, then I'll consider investing in the opportunity... it's that simple. For other people, the first thing you would talk about is how when they join this business and reach a certain level, they can get a company paid BMW, and that would pique their interest.

The point is this, in leadership, you have to first seek to understand people and where they're coming from. You could end up going into a rant about everything that you believe to be true and why you feel your approach to things is the right one. If you don't know who you're speaking to, what drives them, and what they care about, then you are probably wasting words and wasting time. A leader is one of the most critical salespeople on any team because they are selling a vision, whatever that vision is. So as a leader, you have to master the art of asking questions and listening to the answers because you have to make sure you understand who you're talking to. Cedrick was a master at this and knew exactly how to adapt his conversations with people in order for them to see his vision. So it was no surprise that he was able to build a large team of business partners and set himself up in a position where he was able to be self-employed. Conversely, in my 3 months in the business, after talking to hundreds of my family, friends, and co-workers, I didn't sign up a single business partner. Not even one. But guess what, it was completely my fault. From the very beginning, I didn't follow the system that I was taught, and I was so focused on my own personal gain that I wasn't focused on the needs of the people that I was talking to. This is why the first step in the decision-making process is so crucial. If you don't ask the right questions, then you may end up completely misreading a situation.

INTROVERT TURNED PARTY PROMOTER

From the year 2008 through 2011, I was a nightclub promoter in the Dallas and Fort Worth, Texas areas. Now I know what you might be thinking; this guy said he was an introvert; how does someone like that end up choosing to be at parties every weekend surrounded by hundreds of people? Well, at the time, as I was in my late twenties and starting to become more financially stable, I enjoyed being out and exploring what the city had to offer. More importantly, I was interested in an additional source of income and knew several friends that were having success promoting events at that time. So I started out by hosting happy hours with co-workers. At first, it was just to give us somewhere to meet up and connect after work. After a few months of doing this, the word began to spread around Fort Worth, and I was told about someone that was doing similar events in the area. I went to one of his events one night after a friend gave me a copy of his flyer. We introduced ourselves to each other there and exchanged information. Later we talked for hours about our goals and plans for event hosting. That person's name was Mike Carr, who to this day is one of my closest friends. One thing that was clear from meeting him at the event and our follow-up meeting was that he was clearly more extroverted than me. I believe this ended up being extremely beneficial for us, as our personalities were able to balance each other out.

From that point, we became not only business partners but also good friends. We came up with several catchy themes for parties in the Fort Worth and Arlington areas at a time when there were really no other promoters hosting events like ours in those parts of town. There was Fuego

Saturdays at a small restaurant in Fort Worth, First Fridays Arlington, that we would rotate between different hotels and a number of other themed parties. With each event, the number of attendees was growing, we had a core following of people that would come to anything we hosted, but the word was now starting to spread throughout the city as well. Our peak was in late January 2009 when we decided to host an inauguration party for president-elect Barack Obama. We reserved a hotel restaurant and were not really sure of what to expect. The turnout was far greater than we anticipated. Instead of a happy hour setting with 30 to 40 people, we ended up packing out the restaurant to capacity. We received high praise from everyone that attended the event and made a good profit. Riding off of the success of that night, we decided that it was time to scale up.

Right after the success of the inauguration event Mike and I came up with an idea. The restaurant and the other venues where we had been hosting events could accommodate a capacity of between 200 to 300 people on average. What if we doubled the size of the venue? Now we had the potential to have 600 people in attendance. In addition, we would have presale tickets and charge a higher price than we had at our other events. Essentially, we would be looking at a much higher profit potential than what we had seen up to that point. So, what we did was put our money together and reserved the grand ballroom at the Hilton hotel in Arlington, which was right across the highway from Six Flags and the Texas Rangers stadium, a prime location.

After several weeks of promoting the event, fast forward to the morning of. We had only sold 10 pre-sale tickets. A few ticket sales trickled in throughout the day, but at a level that was much less than what we'd anticipated. The evening came, and we both headed to the venue to ensure everything was set up. 8pm quickly came, and we had officially opened doors for the event. As we stood together at the ballroom entrance looking down the empty hotel hallway, we went outside to say a quick prayer. Throughout the night, a few people showed up. We had a well-known DJ, a lavish buffet with an assortment of various gourmet dishes, and multiple bars set up. The people that did come had a great time; the only problem was that there were about 40 of them in total. Financially the event was a significant loss, as we weren't able to recoup our expenses. So, what happened? What did we do wrong? We'll get to that in a minute; before that, here's another quick story.

By the fall of 2010, every event promoter in Dallas was getting ready for the NFL's Superbowl weekend that would be coming to the city in February 2011. By this time, our event promotion business had grown dramatically. We were now doing a weekly Friday night event in Dallas and were routinely partnering with other promoters to do events on Saturday nights as well. The allure of hosting events on Superbowl weekend was clear. There would be people from all over the country in town looking for places to go, and due to this high demand, a promoter could stand to make a lot more income in that one weekend. We teamed up with two other promoters to plan out the events for the weekend. For one of those events, I started looking into various celebrities that we could book to host our event. I came across a booking service out of New York that had a number of athletes and entertainers that were available for booking.

The theme for our Saturday night event was going to be 'Pretty Girls Rock,' and at the time, Rocsi of the BET show 106 and park was well known and liked in the entertainment industry. I called the number on the agency's website, and a fast-talking guy with a heavy New York accent picked up the phone. I told him the details of our event, including the location and the time we needed Rocsi available to attend. He discussed the funds and paperwork needed to book her. It would be 50% of the cost upfront and another 50% on the night when she showed up. I wired the funds to the agency account that day, and within a week, we had Rocsi from 106 and Park on our party flyer. Tickets started selling as soon as we put the event information out, and continued to sell up to the day of the event. Then the weirdest thing happened. A friend of mine called me the morning of the

QUIET VOICE FEARLESS LEADER

event and said they'd watched 106 and Park the day before. They told me that on that show, Rocsi made a comment about going to the Caribbean that weekend and how she couldn't wait to get there.

As I sat there confused, they said, "Isn't she supposed to be at your party tomorrow?" I assured my friend that she would be there, then quickly got off of the phone and called the booking agent. I called him at least 5 times throughout the day and got no response. I was supposed to get a call from him when she landed in Dallas, was on her way to the hotel, and headed to our event. As it got closer to the time for doors to open that evening, it became clear to me that Rocsi was going to be a no-show. I let the other promoters know what was going on, but we didn't announce it. In the end, the night went well, and people had a great time. We didn't make nearly the amount of money that we'd expected, but we did at least make a profit.

The next morning, I called the booking agent again, this time he answered the phone with an apologetic tone. He explained that he was in London, so he had missed several phone calls. His flight would have him back in New York in a few days, and he would wire the funds that I'd sent him to book Rocsi. Well, the day came that he was supposed to arrive back in town and wire the money; I called and got no answer. The next day, I called and texted and got no response. After the third day, I called the company phone number for the booking agency where someone else answered the phone. By this time, I was upset and annoyed; I let them know the situation and that I hadn't received a callback. The lady on the phone was very nonchalant with her response, saying that I should wait another day. At that point, I let her know that if the funds weren't wired by the next day, then I'd be forced to pursue legal action. That seemed to get her attention, and she assured me that everything with the booking agent would be settled and I would have my money before the weekend.

Well, let's see if you can guess what happened next? That's right, I never heard back from him again, and when I called the company phone back a few days later, the number was disconnected. I spoke to a friend of mine who was a lawyer about my options to pursue legal action against them. The amount owed to me was $2,000. In the end, the legal fees, time, and hassle it was going to take to get the money back just didn't seem worth it. So as much as it sucked, I accepted it as a loss, swallowed my pride, and moved on.

So, let's take a minute and analyze each of the scenarios above based on the decision-making method that was discussed in the opening of this chapter. First off, we'll start with the event at the Hilton hotel:

1. Ask Questions and Listen

We had a solid understanding of the venue we had selected for the event. The hotel's event coordinator was excellent, we met, and she gave us every detail that we needed in order to make the night successful. So I believe we had our questions answered going into that night.

2. Understand the Pros and Cons of each decision

Here is the step where we probably could have analyzed further. We spent significant energy focusing on the pros of doing the event – a larger venue will mean a larger crowd and more ticket sales, which will mean more money. A larger event will take our brand to the next level. However, the cons were – what if we're scaling up too fast and don't have the expected turnout? What is the largest financial loss that we could take if the event doesn't go as planned?

3. Make a Decision and Rally the Team behind it

Hindsight is always 20/20; at the time, as two young, ambitious entrepreneurs, there is probably no way that anyone would have talked us out of renting that ballroom. However, looking back, we probably weren't ready at the time. Ironically, within a year, we'd started hosting events in Dallas and we were regularly having events at venues larger than that 600-person ballroom and packing them out. Essentially, we eventually got there.

Booking Rocsi for Superbowl

1. Ask Questions and Listen

This is where I completely dropped the ball. I didn't understand much at the time about booking celebrities for event hosting... take that back; I didn't understand anything about it. I literally found the first website that had a list of celebrities they could book, called the number, talked to the guy, and wired $2,000 the next day. Not only did I not ask him the right questions, but I also didn't do my due diligence in researching his company, which was, in short, me setting us up for failure from the start.

2. Understand the Pros and Cons and make a decision

The major pro, in this case, would've been Rocsi showing up to the event, which would have been great visibility and credibility for our brand. The cons were her not showing up and the potential damage that could've done to our brand, as well as not getting our money back.

3. Make a Decision and Rally the Team Behind It

When I proposed the thought of booking Rocsi to my business partners, everyone was on board and thought it was a great fit with the theme of our event. But ultimately, I put us in a bad position because I didn't ask the right questions upfront.

THREE PILLARS OF COURAGE

ASK THE RIGHT QUESTIONS

In order to make sound decisions as a leader, it's critical that you have a clear understanding of the situation that's in front of you and your team. That understanding can only be gained by asking the right questions. Have you ever rushed to make a decision on something without knowing all of the details? In my 20's I was quick to buy cars, sign up for credit cards and invest in various business ventures with little to no research. My mentality was that if it felt right at the time, why not do it? Needless to say, that rarely turned out well. At one point, I was driving an Infiniti G35 sedan with an insanely high-interest rate because my credit was ruined, had 4 credit cards that were all maxed out, and was taking a monthly loss of over a thousand dollars in my second multi-level marketing business. I could easily write a book about the mistakes made in my 20's alone...no, seriously, I could write a book; maybe that'll be the next one. Anyway, you have to be able to make decisions, sometimes extremely tough decisions, as a leader. So just like Cedrick used to ask several questions when he was talking to somebody to understand them and how to approach them, I had to learn how to ask people the right questions when I was trying to lead them through a difficult situation. Here's a scenario:

You're a project manager at an engineering company. The customer is expecting you to deliver a product to them within the next 6 months; we'll call it widget A. You owe the customer 10 units of widget A, and they've funded you $1 million dollars for the effort (or $100,000 per unit). During the production and test phase of the project, there is an issue discovered where widget A is failing during vibration testing. As vibration levels are increased, there are several screws that are coming loose, and the cover panel that protects the circuit card inside of the widget starts to come loose as well. This is an unacceptable test result for the customer. The production team calls a meeting with you to discuss the issue. During this meeting, one of the design engineers mentions that there is another option; we'll call it widget B. The engineer says that widget B is still going through its preliminary design phase and is being designed to be more rigid than widget A, which means that, in theory, there is a higher chance that it will pass vibration testing. The production team is getting frustrated with all of the failures that widget A is having; by this point, they've tested multiple units, and it appears to be a systemic problem. With that said, the design engineer and production team are all on board with switching over to produce and test 10 widget B units. Since you're the leader, everyone in the room now looks at you, and the design engineer asks, "So are we good to proceed with widget B instead? I can have our engineering team put a rush on finalizing the drawings for widget B and start ordering the material so that we can get this going".

Now you may be saying, well, that's easy. Widget A is having problems, so I chose widget B; that was easy, right? Not so fast, this decision is loaded with questions. First, drawings have been released for widget A, so it has completed its design phase. Units are now being manufactured and going through final testing before delivery. Widget B is still going through design with several engineers working on it. So when will that design be complete? Will there be a formal review of the design, and if so, what happens if something is discovered during the design review and changes have to be made? Is widget B made up of the same materials as widget A? If not, then what is the lead time to get the different materials that are part of widget B shipped to our facility? Is there any cost impact of going with Widget B over Widget A? If the overall cost to deliver widget B is higher than widget A, and it takes longer to deliver, then can the customer live with that? See, that's several questions, and I barely got into the scenario!

A good leader doesn't just make decisions. They have to make **informed** decisions. Asking questions helps to get you the information that you need to make a decision. We'll follow this example through the chapter, but please keep in mind that this same approach is applicable to any field and any situation. If I want to lead a non-profit that helps underprivileged kids, if I want to lead a real estate investment group, if I'm in school and want to lead a group project, then if there's ever a decision to be made, I have to gain a full understanding through asking questions.

UNDERSTAND THE PROS AND CONS

Once you've asked the right questions, now it's time to assess the results of what you've heard. This is where the process can get difficult; in reality, practice and repetition are the only things that allow someone to master this. Depending on the circumstance, you may be able to hear the information, take your notes home, review them over a 2 to 3-day period then come back to the team with a well-thought-out plan. In other cases, there is a widget A unit that is on the assembly line getting ready to enter vibration testing within an hour, an emergency meeting is called, and the team needs to decide whether to proceed or not right now. This is where it becomes critical to now be able to weigh the pros and cons of either option in your decision quickly. The natural approach might be to choose the option that is the quick fix. However, in any decision, it's imperative that you consider both the short and long-term consequences of your decision.

Let's think about personal decisions for a minute, going back to my life as an event promoter. My business partner Mike and I were able to become reasonably successful at consistently bringing out crowds to our events, and it became a solid business for us with consistent income. One aspect of the party promoter lifestyle was that you were usually going to be up late at night. We had a weekly Friday night event from 9pm to 2am and would usually also have a Saturday night event from 9pm to 2am as well. Typically, we would show up early, around 7, to make sure the venue was set up for our event, to make phone calls to people who had reserved tables, and to prepare for the evening. After the party, which would always go a little past 2am, then it was time to count the money that was made at the door. We would pay the DJ, the person that had worked the door, any advertising expenses that were paid for the event, and settle up with the club owner on any revenue from the bar sales. By the time all of this was done, it was normally around 3am. By the time I got home, it was 3:30am. I was 27 when I started hosting events and quit the business a few months after my 30th birthday.

At the time, I didn't have any kids, wasn't married, and could sleep in until noon the next day if I wanted to. Fast forward to today. I'm 40 years old at the time of writing this; I have a 5 and a 3 year old and have been married to my wife for 7 years. Over the past several years, the thought has entered my head (usually a brief thought...like 10 seconds) about the income that our party promotion brand used to bring in and how easy it would probably be to get into the event hosting business again. After all, I still have a lot of the same contacts and have built a strong professional network over the years that I'm sure would support the events. But what are the pros and cons?

Pros – an additional income stream, getting to network and spend time out with friends;

Cons – Time, getting home around 3 in the morning with 2 kids that wake up around 7 every day and need my full attention. In addition, the fact that these days I have no desire to be out every weekend that late.

For me, when I weigh the pros and cons of the club lifestyle, it becomes one that I no longer have any passion or interest in. The fact that those are two pretty big cons makes it an easy decision for me. I still respect and root for the promoters in the Dallas area that I used to work with and love anytime I see them doing well. So, this is not to discredit them or what they do at all. I just had to make a decision for myself and my family.

How do you make decisions in your life? After asking as many questions as necessary to understand the current decision you're looking to make, the next steps of weighing the pros and cons of your decision are critical.

In our earlier example of our widget project being behind schedule, after asking the team several key questions and weighing the pros and cons of proceeding with widget A vs. widget B, the leader is now ready to make a decision. The next and final step is one that is critical to the overall success of the project and is ultimately where the team needs leadership from you the most.

MAKE A DECISION AND RALLY THE TEAM TO BELIEVE IN IT.

Now that you've asked the right questions and weighed the pros and cons of each approach, it's time to make a decision. For some people, regardless of being introverted or extroverted, this is by far the hardest thing to do. Being a decision-maker is what separates true leaders from managers or people that are just assigned a title. When you make a decision, you are signing up for whatever the outcome of that decision will be. And when you are leading a team, the decisions you make not only impact you but your teammates. Obviously, what makes it complicated is that you can't see the future, so you rarely have any way of knowing if your decision will end up working out or not. It can be intimidating, which is why a lot of people prefer to let others make decisions for them. They'll shy away from leadership opportunities, even if they are more than qualified for it, just to avoid this responsibility. But the good news is this... if you've completed steps 1 and 2 properly, then you've made this final step much easier. In my leadership roles, I've found that the more information I'm armed with, the easier it is for me to map out what needs to happen next. You can only get this information by becoming a 'master asker' and weighing the pros and cons of every situation. So now what?

You're in the room, and all eyes are now on you, the leader. The team has answered your questions, you've weighed the pros and cons of going with widget A vs. widget B, and they are ready for you to give direction. The final step for you to take is simple:

Give clear direction to your team with supreme confidence

Two very key words to focus on in that sentence. First is "clear," your direction has to be said in a way where when everyone leaves the room or hangs up from the conference call, there is no confusion about the team's mission. Be extremely detailed, overly detailed if you have to when explaining the team's new direction. In addition, be sure to share with your team why you arrived at the decision that you have made. You may get questions about who, what, where, and why you made the decision. That's fine, and you should address those questions, however, to be clear...you must stand firm in what you believe. If you communicate your decision, then one person asks a question, and you begin to retract what you said, you will come off as indecisive and uncertain. This is why the second word I want to focus on is confidence. Have you ever heard a family member or friend say something and thought to yourself, "Yeah, right, they don't even believe that!". It's no different within the dynamics of a team. Any team needs to be assured that its leader has unwavering confidence and believes 100% in the direction that they are taking them. In short, when you tell your team what you've decided, ensure that you say it with conviction. This takes courage and boldness to do, and guess what...in the end, despite all of your planning and preparation, your decision still might end up being the wrong one. But ultimately, as long as you've weighed all of the factors involved before making your decision, then you can hold your head high regardless of the outcome. Your team will respect your boldness as well. When they see how bold and how confident you are in your decision-making, then they will naturally believe in the mission and believe in you. Will there be someone that will leave the meeting thinking:

"They are out of their mind; widget B will never work! We haven't even finished the design yet. I don't know about this."

Sure, there might be. I have not had 100% agreement on all decisions that I've made in my career as a leader...it just doesn't happen that way. There will always be people with differing opinions, and you'll never make every single person happy, so that shouldn't be your goal. The goal is to do what's best for the team, and as the leader, your decision-making will be the key to ensure this happens.

What Introverts Wish Extroverts knew

Being an introvert, I possess a skill that could be a great asset for you and for any team. That skill is that I spend more time observing than I do talking, which means I also typically spend more time listening. This can be extremely beneficial, and makes me someone that you should put trust in when making difficult decisions. Because I observe and notice things that so many other people don't, I will catch things that you will likely miss. So when it is time to navigate through a tough decision, I've probably already thought about and considered every possible scenario in my head. For that reason, you will definitely want to have me in your corner; when I know that you value my opinion I will go out of my way to help you.

Plan of Action

Ask the right questions – In order to make effective decisions as a leader, you will need to be armed with as much information as possible. What is a challenging decision that you are currently facing in your personal or professional life? Start brainstorming and writing down all of the questions you believe need to be answered in order to make a good decision. Be careful not to write down or even think about solutions at this step yet;

for now, just focus on all of the critical questions that would need to be answered in order for a decision to be made.

Understand the pros and cons of each path – Once you've written down the challenge and all of the questions surrounding it, now start to brainstorm answers to each question that you listed in step 1. Once you have your questions with answers written next to them, now sit back and observe what you've written out. It will quickly become clear that there are different decisions and/or paths that can be chosen as a result of your list. As you identify the potential paths that can be chosen, start to write down the pros and cons of each.

Make a Decision – After writing down questions and applicable answers, as well as reviewing the pros and cons of each decision path, now take a look at all of the factors you've written down. Based on the information in front of you, write down the decision that you believe makes sense for you to make. Take a look at your notes and celebrate for a minute because you've effectively made a decision! This is a practice that you can come back to as many times as you need until it starts to become second nature for you.

CHAPTER 3 – TRUST

"When things go wrong, the team will always look to its leader for strength, to be an anchor they can trust when everyone is surrounded by chaos."

The story of Harriet Tubman has been told countless times and has made her a remarkable figure in American history. In the mid-1800's she is on record as having rescued several slaves from a harsh, inhumane, and detestable life of slavery. Harriet's story has always been inspiring to me. I believe the thing that has always connected with me was her fearlessness, and pure will to fight for the freedom of her people. I could only imagine the bravery it would take to consistently risk your life time and time again to save others. The risk of attempting to escape from the slave plantation was already high enough for one person to attempt himself or herself. The penalty for attempting to run away was being beaten with a whip or being lynched from the nearest tree as an example for other slaves to see. Not only did Harriet escape the Maryland plantation that she was raised on with her life, she then decided to risk it all and go back to help others escape for freedom. Most historical records state that she took over 13 trips and freed over 70 slaves during that time period. It's not like she was just telling slaves how to escape; she was taking every single trip with them. So, every time she would leave to pick up more slaves to bring to freedom, she went with the intention of taking the same risk they were taking. She didn't show up and say:

"Alright, so listen, here's a map. Follow the arrows, ask for these people along the way, and in 3 weeks, you'll be free."

Harriet didn't do that because she knew that in order for the slaves she rescued to truly find freedom, they would have to be led. And that meant her walking and running step by step with them, each and every time. The secret route to freedom was known as the Underground Railroad, where there were safe houses along the way for slaves to take refuge along the journey. Her nickname was Moses, and she is credited for saying that despite the threat of sure death, she never lost a 'passenger' that came along the journey with her. Harriet was willing to risk it all while fighting for the freedom of others, and that is why she'll always be one of my role models for true leadership.

Are you willing to fight for the people on your team? Are you willing to do the same work that you would ask others to do? To achieve any goal worth achieving, it takes a persistent work ethic, and it takes courage. Sometimes the work can be extremely grueling, frustrating, and time-consuming. Some leaders of teams will see the hard work coming and immediately begin to assign all of that work to other people. Sure they may take on the easy tasks, the low-hanging fruit that doesn't require them to roll up their sleeves and get in the trenches. But for the more challenging tasks, they'll avoid the responsibility and give that burden to someone else. In that type of leader's mind, this means that if anything goes wrong during the execution of the task, they get to divert the blame to the person who was assigned to work on it. It's a very short-sighted and individualistic approach to take when working on a team.

In contrast, consider the leader that takes the opposite approach. When the team is faced with a difficult scenario and doesn't know which way to turn, the leader's first thought is to roll up their sleeves and get in the trenches with them. The leader doesn't point out the flaws in what everyone else has been doing or start assigning out tasks while sitting in the comfort of their office as the team gets the work done. Instead, whatever the problem is, they are actively engaged in working with the team toward a solution. You'll see this leader involved in brainstorming discussions with the team, talking about various options for overcoming the effort that's in front of them. If a team meeting starts at 8am, they've already been online 30 minutes before to work on the issue, talking to other team members, and going out of their way to help others on the team to remove any obstacles they've been facing. Over time an interesting thing typically starts to happen with leaders of teams that operate like this. Inevitably, they will begin to build trust with their teammates, and those teammates will do whatever they can to work with that leader. The opposite is also true; when the leader doesn't want to get in the trenches with his or her team, it doesn't go unnoticed. Over time that team begins to lose a level of respect for that person and ultimately stops following them.

One thing to note, don't take this principle to mean that an effective leader should be involved in doing everything for the team. That's not what I'm saying at all. It's extremely important for a leader to learn the art of leveraging their teams through delegation, especially as those teams grow in size (we'll discuss more on delegation in a later chapter). This is simply saying that a true leader isn't afraid to get their hands dirty and to fight for their people. When there is hard work to be done, the first person that should be raising their hand to volunteer to help solve the problem at hand should be the leader. Other people notice this behavior, and it solidifies the fact that the leader is not caught up in their title or position. They just want to get the job done and will back up anyone on the team as necessary. This not only helps to achieve the team goals but also leads to other people wanting to step up to be leaders as well.

MOM - THE FIGHTER

When I was in the 3rd grade, around 9 years old, I started getting in trouble at school. The teacher would get on me for talking too much in class and disrupting the other students while they were trying to do their work.

I was a pretty hyper kid; I loved sports, loved building things, and was always moving around looking for something to get into. After about a month or so of problems in class, my teacher put me in what was called the "attitude adjustment" program. Whenever she felt like I'd had a good day and behaved better, I would get a happy sticker. If I had a bad day and was disruptive, I would get a sad face.

We had just moved to the southern California area, and my mom wasn't working at the time. In her career as an educator, she'd been offered opportunities to be a school principal several times, but she declined every time because she preferred to stick with her passion, which was teaching music. So, my mom was well versed in the education field and in how to deal with kids of all age ranges. As part of the attitude adjustment system, my parents were supposed to punish me if I'd had a bad day and reward me if I'd had a good day. There were many days when I remember my mom picking me up from school, and I would walk toward the car with my head down because I knew I'd gotten a bad report. We would get home, and eventually, my dad would come home from work, and I'd have to tell him that I'd had a bad day as well. It got to the point where I started trying to hide my reports because I just didn't want to deal with letting my parents down constantly. The reports normally used to say that I talked loudly and disrupted the class. It also said that I always finished my work quickly.

My mom began talking to my dad about it and how she felt it was a sign that I wasn't being challenged by the work. She started calling the school and asking my teacher questions about the reports I was getting. After listening to a variety of excuses and explanations, she realized that something about the answers she was getting just didn't make sense. After a while, my mom got frustrated with the process. She volunteered to become a school mom, which meant she would come in to help the teacher in our class on certain days. So, the school approved my mom to come in and help out. What my mom didn't tell them was that she was a former winner of the teacher of the year award in multiple school districts and that she held a master's degree in education. On the first day of her volunteering, she showed up dressed normally, very unassuming. She came to class and just said, "Hey, I'm here to help." The teacher actually didn't know that my mom was coming, so it took her by surprise, but she welcomed the help. During my mom's first day of volunteering, I finished my work early like I normally would, so I sat there looking around while the other kids were still working. My mom noticed this and whispered to the teacher, "Hey, I think Terry is done with his work; can I hand him something else to do?" The teacher handed her another assignment, which my mom brought over to me, and I began to work on it. The new assignment kept me busy, and everything was fine.

The next day the teacher didn't expect my mom to come back. My mom decided to come back around the middle of the day unannounced, just to observe the dynamics of the class on a regular day. When my mom got to the classroom, there were kids acting up, being loud, running in circles, and everything in between. The teacher actually had her back to the door as my mom watched. The teacher pointed at a few kids and casually said, "Hey, stop being silly," with a calm tone and demeanor. Then I laughed extremely loud at a friend's joke and immediately heard the teacher shout emphatically, "Terry Lee! Go sit in the corner now!" My mom had caught her in that moment without the teacher realizing it. She backed away and walked away from the classroom. That night, of course, I came home with a frowny face and a bad report. On that day, my mom had enough; she had seen what she needed to see.

She scheduled a meeting with the school principal for that week. To start off the meeting, she let the principal know that she was an experienced educator and informed them of her credentials. The principal was shocked. This clearly was not someone who had randomly shown up to volunteer for a day. She let them know her observations of the teacher and of the situation with me. She said that from what she saw, I needed to be challenged more and also that I could be loud and was active but was also being treated differently. When the teacher asked me to stop doing something, I stopped, but when the other kids were asked the same thing, they didn't stop and also weren't a part of the "attitude adjustment" program. She asked the principal what could be done; at the time, the school was recommending that I be prescribed ridelin to calm me down from being so hyper. But my mom wasn't about to allow that to happen. She asked if I could take an aptitude test just to see where I stood. The principal agreed to it, and we were given a date for the test.

Fast forward to the results of the test coming in. I completely aced it. My mom received a call from the principal, very embarrassed and expressing her apologies for what had happened, and the process started to have me transferred to a gifted and talented program at another school. The conversation that my mom looked forward to was with the teacher that had been giving me bad reports and frowny faces all of those months. Of course, the teacher didn't want to talk to my mom and never did. I got to the new school and found myself in a completely different situation. The kids there were learning how to play chess, were reading much more advanced books, and were learning at a faster pace. Within my first few months, I started to receive several academic awards; it was a warm environment that encouraged and challenged me.

My mom saw something that I wasn't able to see. The reason I was acting out in my other classroom was that I was bored. I would get my work done faster than most of the other kids then I'd be looking for something to do. I simply wasn't being challenged. Sadly this happens all of the time in the school system. I can only imagine how many young boys and girls have been written off as disruptive, class clowns, and unable to learn, when in reality, given the right environment are brilliant minds. This is a big reason that I'm so passionate about society never giving up on a kid and why I love mentoring so much. I often think about what trajectory my life might have taken if my mom had not fought for me through that. Me taking that test did something for me. I went from believing I was the bad kid in the class that couldn't get anything right at school or at home to believing that I was smart and was special. It planted a seed in me, and sometimes that's all you need. That simple thought carried with me for the rest of my life, and it wouldn't have happened if my mom hadn't fought for me.

BOYCOTT

In the summer of 2007, several of my co-workers and I had become good friends and were hanging out regularly. At the time, we would routinely meet up at various locations for happy hours, where we would spend hours laughing, sharing stories, and having conversations about topics as wide-ranging as politics, dating, music, and a million other things. This particular summer, our new place to hang out was a Mexican restaurant just south of downtown Fort Worth (FYI, I'm purposely leaving the name of the restaurant out of this story...). Every Friday after work from 5pm to around 8 or 9, we would all meet there to have drinks and a good con-versation. It initially started out small, around 4 to 5 people. Over time additional people started to be invited, and the size of the group even-tually grew. Also, the word began to spread beyond our group about this restaurant's happy hour being the place to be on Fridays. Every week it was packed with people. The majority of the people in our group were black. There were very few black employees working at the company at that time. We found ourselves bonding due to many of us having similar backgrounds. That will become relevant to the story here in a minute....

One day we all were hanging out on a Friday evening. There was noth-ing different or special about this particular day. Our group was between 12 to 15 people in size sitting at multiple tables near the restaurant's bar area. One of our friends that were there with us happened to be standing near our table watching the football game. While he was standing there, another guy, walking quickly and seeming incoherent, bumped shoulders with the guy in our group. And when I say bumped shoulders, it was not light or unnoticeable. Immediately the guy that had walked by and bumped shoulders with our friend started yelling and cursing him out. He was clearly drunk and was loud. Everyone within ten feet started to look over at what was happening. To his credit, our friend was extremely calm, especially considering the words that were being yelled in his face. A few of us got up from our seats, attempting to do either one of two things 1) de-escalate the situation or 2) defend our friend if things got physical. The exchange lasted less than a minute, and the man eventually stumbled and walked away from our section.

We all sat down, talking about what had just happened, and went back to what we were doing. About five minutes later, we looked up, and the general manager of the restaurant was standing at our table. What he said next was completely unexpected. He stated that there had been a complaint about our section, and we were being asked to leave. We all explained the scenario and what happened to our friend, that the guy who was actually the aggressor and had bumped him was being loud and causing a scene. We were actually at our tables, minding our business. Well, that didn't matter, the general manager repeated that we had to leave the restaurant. Each of us tabbed out and got our checks, feeling completely disrespected and unheard. To add insult to the situation, the guy who had started the altercation was allowed back in the restaurant and walked past us as we exited!

Over the next few days, my friends and I kept talking about what had happened. We knew for sure what the optics were of a black male at a crowded restaurant being in a confrontation, and having 3 tables of black people behind him. Sadly, we were viewed as the aggressors, as the ones that had caused a problem, regardless of what the truth was. So they saw it easiest to ask us to leave. Clearly, we wouldn't be going back to that restaurant anymore; that much was certain. But that just wasn't enough for us. Ironically a significant portion of the patrons that had started coming to the restaurant on Fridays were black—specifically, young professionals living in the Fort Worth area. We wanted to make sure that people were aware of what had happened; we couldn't just let the situation pass.

So, the following week I drafted up an email. The email described every detail about the incident that happened and named the restaurant with the restaurant's address. In conclusion, I stated that I'd no longer be supporting their business. One morning I sent the email to my group of friends and co-workers in Fort Worth, at that time, around 30 people, and went on with my day. What happened next was nothing short of amazing. Within a few days, I had various coworkers and friends from other parts of the city reaching out to me asking about what happened because they had received a copy of the email. At work, I would have people stop me in the halls to ask me about it. Within a week, a friend of mine sent me a forwarded email with the title 'Boycott (restaurant name).' When I opened the email, it was my message with my name at the bottom. So, the message had been forwarded so many times that it made its way back to me! Well, somehow, the email actually made its way to someone at the restaurant. I received a call from a person on the restaurant staff about coming to meet with them. After much thought, my friends Shana, Naida, and I decided to meet with the general manager and others. That evening, they tried to explain their version of what happened that day, offered their apologies, and offered to give a few free meals to us if we returned. I can't remember every word of what was said during the meeting, but the truth is the damage had already been done. Even if we wanted to reverse what happened, the incident had become the talk of the city. As weeks went by, when I would drive past the restaurant, I noticed fewer and fewer cars in the parking lot. The Friday evenings that used to be packed with people were now quickly dwindling. Within a year, I'll never forget driving by the restaurant and seeing that it had closed down.

Now look, I'm not saying that the boycott that my friends and I led was the sole cause for the restaurant closing. But I will say that there is a strong chance that it had something to do with it. I also have to be honest and say that I never sent that email with the intention to see their business shut down. I simply wanted people to be aware of the situation that happened. See, I'm a very level-headed and calm person. One thing, however that gets to me is when I feel that someone is disrespecting my family or my friends. At that moment, I just felt that our friend had been disrespected, and we had all been disrespected at a restaurant where we had spent our hard-earned dollars for several months. This is another example of fighting for what you believe in and fighting for your people. It won't always be the convenient thing to do, but it is necessary.

THREE PILLARS OF TRUST

SOLVE YOUR TEAM'S BIGGEST PROBLEMS

When is the last time you wrote down a plan for anything, and it ended up going exactly how you'd planned it? If you're among the almost non-existent group of people in this world that has always had everything go right in your life, then kudos to you. You're rare and possibly not human! For the large majority of us that make plans and set goals for ourselves, we know that these plans will oftentimes change. In all of the programs that I've worked in my career, the one thing that remains constant is change. Sometimes change can be in your favor. Other times, change can cause the project that you're working on to be derailed and possibly even fail. Being a leader when everything is going well, all schedule milestones are being met, and the team is getting along great is one thing. What happens when you've been asked to lead a team, and your team is behind schedule by several months, your allocated budget for a project has been overspent, and you have people on the team that are constantly at odds with each other? How does one lead through that scenario?

One thing that I've made a habit of doing recently in my career is to write down the hardest issues that need to be solved on a particular day. I look at that list and immediately begin to prioritize. What are the things that absolutely have to get done today? Those items are the first to get my attention. From there, I try to have a plan and set deadlines for the remaining list items. Once I know the most critical actions for the day, the question now becomes this: What can I do to help with this situation right now? In many cases, the problem that has to be solved is a hard one and not exactly clear. It is during these times that you have the opportunity to use your unique abilities to think creatively toward a solution.

A common reaction by many people when things go wrong is to complain, to blame others, or to avoid responsibility. And if we're honest with ourselves, most of us have probably done at least one of those three before. But the reality is; we don't have time for that! When you're a leader, the rules change. When things go wrong, the team will always look to its leader for strength, to be an anchor they can trust when everyone is surrounded by chaos. So when the trouble comes (not if, but when…), what are you going to do about it? If your team has a school project that needs to be done by the end of the week, it's already Wednesday, and one of the people on the team hasn't done their part, are you going to talk about them behind their back and blame the project being late on them? Or will you offer to do that person's part of the project, help direct the team on what needs to be completed next, and progress forward? If you have a business and a shipment of your product is late, which has caused your deliveries to your customers to be late, will you send an email to your customers bad-mouthing the supplier and blaming them for your late deliveries? Or will you figure out a way to expedite the shipment with your suppliers and work to make up for the late deliveries with your customers?

When things go wrong, and you are the leader, you have a clear choice. Personally, I love being surrounded by people that are problem solvers. These are the kind of people that you need to have around you whenever things go wrong. So naturally, if I'm going to call myself a leader, then I need to ensure that I'm helping to solve problems as well. When the team knows that their leader is not just talking about doing something to help a situation but is also actively working on it, another level of trust is built. Now when the leader is speaking, the team feels invested because they know that leader is willing to get in the trenches with them and battle against the hard problems.

THE TEAM TAKES ON THE PERSONALITY OF ITS LEADER

What is your first reaction when you get some bad news? Depending on how bad the news is, some people might get angry, worried, stressed, fearful, or a number of other emotions. Have you ever had a significant other break up with you, and you had no idea it was coming? I remember this happening to me and feeling my chest tighten to the point that I thought

I was about to have a heart attack, and I was in my late 20's at the time. What about feeling overwhelmed? A middle school or high school student that's living at home might feel overwhelmed by trying to balance school-work with extra-curricular activities, trying to meet the standards of their parents at home, and trying to figure out the next steps for his or her life when they become an adult. Or maybe you're in a career where you find yourself constantly balancing time between work or business, your family, your friends, various social groups, and somewhere in between all of that, trying to find time for yourself. It can be a lot just going through the daily grind of life, so when bad news comes in on top of that, it can be a tremendous burden. But ironically, this is when some leaders excel.

Let's say your business has a live event scheduled where over 300 people have purchased tickets, and 2 weeks before the event, the venue calls and tells you that they have to cancel due to unforeseen circumstances. So what now? You have 10 people that have been helping you to coordinate this event for the past several months, and in 2 weeks, you know that there is a chance you could end up with 300 customers that will never support your event-planning brand again. When the word about the canceled event starts to spread on social media, then those 300 unhappy people could turn into negative publicity in front of thousands. Some people in this situation would respond by cursing the venue owner out on the phone and would demand that they allow them to have the event. Others might call a meeting with their team and start talking about all of their concerns, how they don't know how to pull the event together now, and of course, spend over an hour talking about how wrong the venue is for canceling on them at the last minute like that. But another person would take the phone call from the venue, hear the bad news, and immediately start thinking about solutions. Once they've had a chance to think about solutions, they would then present those solutions to their team for feedback. From those discussions, they would then quickly act on any alternatives that were presented.

If there's one thing that I've learned after observing hundreds of leaders and now being in leadership positions myself, it's that people are always watching the actions and behaviors of the leader. When things go wrong, is the leader acting scared? Is the leader too timid to make a decision? Is the leader spending so much time complaining about what went wrong that they're losing precious time to come up with a solution? Does the leader lack confidence when they're communicating? If the leader exhibits any of the traits described above, then so will the team. The leader is supposed to be the anchor that holds the ship at bay, regardless of the storms that threaten to tear the team apart. If the leader is not strong, then the team is basically on a ship with no anchor, so when the storms come, there will be pure chaos, and every wind will pull the team in any direction. Another trap that is easy to fall into is to do nothing or to not have a sense of urgency when problems arise. Sometimes when things get hard, it feels easier to throw in the towel:

"Well, we tried, maybe next time."

This type of apathetic response will be picked up by the team and is a hard mindset to break once it's been formed. The common attitude will become:

"Well, our leader's not that worried about it, why should we?"

This is the last thing you want to happen because you have now created a culture where people are not on fire for the mission of the team, and in the worst case, they don't even care. So lack of action can never be the response. If we are leaders, then our assignment is to be the first ones to take action when times get hard. Our teammates will see this and will naturally do the same. And the best part is that it doesn't take being an extrovert to do this. What it takes is a mindset that is focused on action and results and the ability to provide calmness to your team even when circumstances seem to not warrant that. Regardless of what is going on, when your team sees how relaxed and confident you are when everything around you seems to suggest that you shouldn't be, they will also be that way. This is another great way to build trust, as they will start to admire how you handle adversity. My suggestion is to figure out the type of leader that you want to be because the storms will most definitely come, and you can be the anchor that holds everyone together.

BAD NEWS DOESN'T GET
BETTER WITH TIME

When I first started my role as a project engineer at a prior company, I spent several months being mentored and coached by other engineers on the team. One of the phrases that my mentor Chris Byrd told me that always stuck with me was that "bad news doesn't get better with time." The way he explained it to me is that when things go wrong if you knew about it for months and didn't tell anyone, when they find out later they'll be 100 times as upset and bothered by it. Had you let them know what was going on upfront, then they would have had time to adjust their expectations and offer you suggestions for a different approach. Instead, if you wait to tell them now, you might be too far down the path to do anything to change it. Not to mention the fact that you have likely lost some trust with them. So why does this matter, and what are some examples of this? If you're reading this book and you were born in the 1980s or prior like me, then you remember when your report card would get mailed to your house from school. Depending on how your grades were at some point, you might have been the first to check the mail every day because you didn't want your parents to see your grades. This only started becoming an issue for me around the 8th and 9th grade, when I had the brilliant idea (insert sarcastic air quotes..) to purposely sabotage my grades so that I would be accepted by my friends and not be looked at as a nerd. We'll talk more about that later.

Anyway, even if you got the report card out of the mail before your parents intercepted it, you knew at some point they were going to ask where the grades were anyway. So it was pointless; at most, you might buy yourself a week before you would have to address it. Another example of this would be if the team lead at your job asked for a status on your project, and you know that it's been running behind schedule by several weeks. You have the choice of letting them know that ahead of time or waiting to tell them on the day that it's due that it will take another 2 weeks. So if we know the pitfalls of delaying bad news, then why do we do it? Most likely, it's because we're afraid. Afraid of the backlash that might be received, afraid of the possible confrontation, or maybe afraid of disappointing someone. These are all-natural emotions to feel, and because many introverts prefer to avoid confrontation, that can make this even more difficult. But the truth is that these emotions are rooted in fear, and a huge component of leadership is to break down any potential sources of fear in your life. And that's all withholding negative information is; an action that is done out of fear.

To be effective leaders, we have to flip that and lead from a space of fear-lessness. Instead of being the kid that is afraid to show their bad grades, go ahead and show them, then take responsibility for any bad grade received where you could have worked harder. Instead of being afraid to talk to the project lead about your task being late, let them know where you stand as soon as possible and give them the real reasons for why. Regardless of the response you receive, you will feel so much better knowing that you've been open and honest with the truth. As a project manager where I am actively monitoring cost and schedule performance for a large number of tasks on a multi-million-dollar program, I have been given bad news many times. I've been on the other end, where I'm the one delivering bad news as well. It comes with the territory and is not a foreign concept at all in our industry. I can say firsthand that when I'm told upfront about a technical issue, a task being behind schedule, or something being over budget, it is always better to know as soon as it happens. There is also a feeling of relief, as strange as it might sound when I'm made aware of something that's gone wrong, and I immediately inform the people that need to know. The longer the information sits and is untold, the more the weight of it continues to grow. The alternative of holding it in oftentimes backfires and just isn't worth it. Ultimately, leaders don't run from the harsh reality that the truth can bring; they embrace it and learn to lead through it. To fight for your team being upfront and direct with any news (positive or negative) is critical.

What Introverts Wish Extroverts knew

As an introvert, I can be extremely loyal and will fight for the people that I care about. In many cases, although I might have several associates, I most likely keep the circle of people that I share my true self with much smaller. So character traits like loyalty and trust are extremely important for me. If you show me that you are a loyal person, and if I know that I can trust you to do what you say, then I will undoubtedly be one of the greatest assets to your team. However, when I begin to doubt your loyalty, and am unsure if I can trust you enough to share my thoughts with you; then you will most likely only get to know me at a surface level.

Plan of Action

Solve Your Team's Biggest Problems - Write down an issue or problem that someone on your team or your team as a whole is currently having. It doesn't have to be a major problem, but it can be. Either way, write down what the problem is and start to brainstorm ideas for ways that you might be able to help fix it. You don't necessarily have to be the person that solves the issue; your action might be to simply introduce someone to someone else that can solve their problem. The point here is to be of service to your team and make solving their problem your highest priority. The key is to follow-up until the action is complete, so plan to begin the process of helping but ensure you are available to see it through.

The team takes on the personality of the leader – Write down at least 5 leaders that you know and admire. This could be someone at work, in your business, your local church, a friend, family member, or others. Preferably it should be people that you interact with frequently enough to observe how they carry themselves on a consistent basis. Now think about and write down a few positive observations that you notice about each person's personality. Take some time to reflect on the traits you've written down. Now take some time to reflect on yourself, and ask the question: 'If everyone on my team acted like me, would our team be successful?' That is a question that only you can answer. If you feel good about the answer, then give yourself a pat on the back. You're on the right track. If you find that you don't like the answer to that question, it's ok. It just means that this is a great time to work on growing yourself into the leader that you would like to be.

Bad News Doesn't get better with time – Is there any bad news that you've been preventing yourself from telling a co-worker, business partner, spouse, significant other, child, or anyone else? If so, write it down, and make the decision to tell them today. Depending on how bad the news is, I realize this might be extremely difficult. But this will help in starting to form the habit of sharing bad news quickly and effectively. I have held secrets in about a number of things at various times in my life. People equate the moment that you confess something you were hiding with the feeling of a weight being lifted. I can say that is exactly what it has felt like for me in the past. Whatever that thing is, whether professional or personal, go ahead and get it out. Everyone involved will be better off for it.

Chapter 4
– Accountability

"Leaders don't point the finger at others, and leaders don't throw in the towel when things don't execute to plan. Leaders take personal responsibility first, then come up with a plan to redirect and execute."

"**S**orry I wasn't able to get my homework done. I forgot it was due today."

"*My fault that I'm late for our meeting.*"

"*I know I said I would call you back. I've just been too busy.*"

"*You know I'm going to write my book one day, whenever I get the time.*"

"*My boss doesn't like me, and I think one of my coworkers has been sabotaging me. That's why I haven't got my promotion yet.*"

"*My idea will turn into the next big thing. Just wait and see! As soon as I get these investors to believe in it, then I'll start*"

Have you heard or said any of these before? Most likely, you have because it's a common language. It's a language that is universally spoken and has been around forever. It is the language of excuses. I'm a big believer in the power of words, that what comes out of our mouths begins to manifest our reality in the world. What are we communicating to others when we give excuses, how does that impact the way that other people perceive us? Or think of it this way; ask yourself what do you think of people that regularly have excuses for everything? You know the people where nothing is ever their fault; it was always someone or something else. Well, I can tell you what I think. In my experience, people like that are often not reliable and may lack the ability to take responsibility for their actions. Both of these are traits that are extremely important for me to have in a relationship with someone, whether business or personal.

Now don't get me wrong, life happens. If you told a friend that you'd come to their kid's birthday party, your tire catches a nail on the street, and now you're sitting on the side of the road with a flat tire, then that is just life happening. When you have a deadline to meet at work or in your business, someone in your family gets ill, and you need to shift priorities to care for them. That is life happening. But when you have a friend or family member that's going through a rough time and could really benefit from getting a call from you, if every time you're about to call, you convince yourself that you're too busy...that's an excuse. When you have an idea for a new business or an idea that could change the way your team operates at work, but you tell yourself that you can start working on it tomorrow...that's an excuse, and you're making assumptions. Not to be morbid, but who promised that you would even be here tomorrow? When we look at it that way, it starts to change our view of every decision and every encounter.

By the way, the reason I can speak on this topic is that I can be a terrible procrastinator and, in my life, I have made several excuses whenever bad things would happen. Case in point, I had the concept to write this book over 3 years ago, and you're just now reading it. Every time I would start to put words on a page, here's what I would tell myself:

"Your story's really not that impressive or inspiring. Listen to the story of (insert name). They have over a million followers on social media. You're not at that level."

"You're not as exciting as (insert name) when you speak. They are a master story-teller, take command of a room, and are great communicators. You're too relaxed, you're not the life of the party or that exciting. Why would anyone want to listen to you?"

"You know, life is just too busy, and life is good. You have an amazing wife, two kids, and your career is going well. You don't really need to write a book anyway. Besides there's just no time."

These are examples of the excuses that I would say to myself. Any inspiration that I had to start writing would slowly wither away with every word of self-doubt until eventually I would close my laptop and forget about writing that day. I wonder if I'm the only one, or if someone reading this might be able to relate. Take a hard look at yourself and think about it. During a typical week, as you encounter various situations, do you find yourself making excuses for your behavior and actions often? How about the people around you? This isn't a question that I can answer for you. You'll have to truly dig deep and think about it.

So why does this matter, and why is an excuse-free mindset so critical to your ability to lead? The answer is simple; leaders must be willing and able to take accountability at all times. There are not many things in this world that bother me or get me upset, and when I say not many, I mean literally almost nothing. One thing that does bother me is when I hear someone blame everyone else in the world for his or her problems. You know the person that seems to always have something negative to say about other people, and anytime they're going through something, it's everybody's fault but their own. Because, of course, it never has anything to do with something they did! When we start to shift our mindset away from the language of excuses, a strange thing will happen. When we're around a group of people that are constantly complaining, blaming others for their problems, and making excuses, it will start to make us uncomfortable. Progressing further into this mindset, you'll find that you really don't want to spend time around these people unless absolutely necessary. Conversely, when you meet and interact with people who are accountable for their mistakes, taking action on their goals, and encouraging others, then you'll be drawn to that. Remember, from earlier in the book, a team will take on the personality of its leader. You don't want to be known as the leader who makes excuses and blames other people anytime things go wrong. If you do, then your team's culture will follow suit. The great thing about life is that you have the power to change and to adapt. If you've never made an excuse for anything in your life, then God bless and continue what you've been doing. For those of us that have, which I suspect to be the majority, let this be the day that we commit to never make excuses again.

THE COLLEGE "ALMOST" GRADUATE

In the fall of 2004, I was so ready to graduate from college. I loved FAMU. I'd made lifelong friends and unforgettable memories there. But it was now time to get out into the world and transition into the next phase of life. A week before graduation day, my parents, my sister, my grandmother, uncles, aunts, and cousins living in Tallahassee were all planning to attend the ceremony. We had just completed final exams for all of our classes; my classmates and I that were going to be graduating were so excited. Getting through an Electrical Engineering major had been challenging, and I felt a huge sense of accomplishment to get to that point. A few days after the last exams, final grades were released for the semester. I was confident that I had done well in all of my classes, except for one that I wasn't sure about.

It was my Electromagnetic Fields class with Dr. Arora. Out of all the classes I took in my major, this one proved to be the hardest for me. A few days before graduation, I drove up to the engineering school to check on my grades. The teachers would typically post grades on their office door for us to see. I walked up to Dr. Arora's office and saw all of the other students huddled outside of his door. I began scanning the grade sheet to look for my student ID number and my grade. I found my student ID, and next to it was a D which was a failing grade. My mouth dropped in shock, and I stood there for a minute in disbelief. Several of the other students that were standing there had also received a low grade. We all shared the same feelings of despair and disbelief at that moment. I knocked on his door, and several other students were doing the same. There was no answer, but we all assumed he was there. After several minutes he eventually cracked the door open but did not open it fully. The other students and I began pleading:

"Dr. Arora, can we please talk about my grade? Is there anything that I can do? I'm supposed to graduate."

Honestly, I don't remember his exact response to us, but the short version of the answer was "No." He closed the door in our faces, and we all just stood there stunned. What this meant was that I could walk at the graduation ceremony in a few days, but I would not receive my bachelor's degree due to this failing grade. So, although my entire family was coming to celebrate my graduation, I wasn't actually going to be graduating. I would have to call my parents before their flight from Dallas to Tallahassee to let them know what had happened, one of the hardest calls I would ever have to make in my life. I paced around my room, feeling sick to my stomach, with no idea of what to say. I delayed and delayed, and finally, the day before they were going to board the flight, I called my mom and dad. With my voice trembling, I told them about the failing grade. Filled with shame, I felt like I'd let my entire family down. They ended up coming, as did the rest of my family, and I did walk across the stage. But in many ways, it was an empty feeling, I walked, but I knew I hadn't accomplished my goal.

Now at the time, I had several people to blame and a lot of excuses to make for this outcome. I blamed Dr. Arora for giving me the D, and I blamed how hard my major was. I even blamed the weather! There was one night where there was a hurricane watch in Tallahassee, and they had predicted the hurricane would hit the following day. So, our assumption was that school would be canceled that next morning, and we wouldn't be taking our scheduled Electromagnetic Fields exam. So I didn't study that night for it (never mind the fact that I should've been studying for weeks leading up to the test and not waiting until the night before...). The next day

I woke up, and the sun was out with not one cloud in the sky. Needless to say, I didn't do well on that test, and that didn't help my final grade in the end.

Eventually, I had to face the truth. The truth was that I deserved that D; that was the level of effort I'd put in, so that's what I got in return. Period, no excuses. At the time, I was heavily involved in my fraternity, working in multiple positions, was partying with my friends and frat brothers throughout the week, and was spending a lot of time with my girlfriend. With the type of major that I had, it was going to require a dedicated and laser-sharp focus to succeed. And that semester, I didn't have it. After walking the stage, I had fellow classmates that were getting ready to start new careers as engineers at fortune 500 companies making great salaries. Meanwhile, I packed up everything in my room, left Tallahassee, and headed back to Dallas with no job and no degree. One of the first things I did was enrolled in an Electromagnetic Fields course at the University of Texas Arlington for the spring 2005 semester. I also started applying for any and every job that I could find. I was now going to be staying at my parent's house, in my old room, until I could figure out how to get on my feet. It was humbling, to say the least. I started working at a call center, making a little over minimum wage. I would attend my class in the day and would work at the call center at night. But this time, when I was sitting in class, I was focused. I spent countless hours in the school library, at tutoring sessions on campus, and at home studying. I was rarely going out with friends or socializing. I had removed any distractions that I felt would keep me from doing well in the class.

Fast forward to the end of the semester. I walked to the professor's office to review my final grade, the same walk I'd made to Dr. Arora's office 5 months earlier. I scanned the paper that was posted on the professor's door, and next to my student ID was a B+. I breathed a huge sigh of relief. A deep satisfaction came over me because I knew that I'd given everything that I had. About a week or so later, my school transcripts were updated, paperwork was processed, and in the spring of 2005, I "officially" became a college graduate with a B.S. degree in Electrical Engineering.

I used to think sometimes about how much easier my life would've been if I'd just passed Dr. Arora's class. I would have avoided an extra semester of school (and an extra semester of college tuition...which I had to pay out of pocket), would have avoided walking across the stage at my alma mater in front of thousands of people knowing I hadn't graduated and would have avoided moving back in with my parents while my friends were now driving luxury cars with their own apartments. But ultimately, it is a part of my story, and it taught me a powerful lesson. When we fall down, we can get up and make progress, or we can lie down and make excuses. There is no middle ground. Leaders don't point the finger at others, and leaders don't throw in the towel when things don't execute to plan. Leaders take personal responsibility first, then come up with a plan to redirect and execute. I had to learn this the hard way.

FRED LEE SR. – QUIET STRENGTH

In 1951, my grandfather, Fred Lee Sr. became the first African American police officer in the city of Tallahassee, Florida. At the time, the city was segregated, so the areas where each of my parent's families lived were predominately black. I never got to meet granddad Fred as he had passed away before I was born. But growing up, I would hear stories about him all the time that made me feel as if I knew him. He was not a small man by any means, six foot three, stocky, built like a defensive lineman with large hands. He grew up in Panama City, Florida, with nine other brothers and one sister. From all the stories that I heard, the Lee men were notorious for being a group of characters. They were well known around Panama City and by the rest of the family for always talking, arguing, laughing, and cracking jokes on each other. As popular as they were, out of the brothers, my grandfather had a reputation for being the quiet one.

He eventually made his way to Tallahassee and started working as a cook at Leon High School. At the time, leaders in the community began talking to city officials about a plan to integrate the city's police department. The city asked for names of candidates, and my grandfather was one of three that were chosen; at the time, he was 38 years old. Out of the three men, two of them quit before being hired, leaving my grandfather as the only black police officer in the city. As he began his career, he was assigned to patrol the Frenchtown area, a predominately black section of the city. At the time, he was the only police officer in his department that didn't have a squad car, so he would patrol his area on foot. In fact, if he was arresting a white man during his shift, he had to call another police officer to come to pick the person up. He experienced true racism, especially during his early days as a police officer, which was a reason that my grandmother had reservations about him taking the job, to begin with. I'm sure there are details about what he went through that I'll never know, but given that it was the 1950's in the deep south, I can only imagine. The level of pressure and stress that he endured on a daily basis had to be extreme. Despite this, my grandfather was never one to complain and never one to give up. And the community of Frenchtown loved and respected him.

People knew him as a man of few words, but when he spoke, people listened. I would hear stories growing up from my dad and others about times where there would be someone drunk in the street or a fight would break out. My grandfather would show up, and instead of being aggressive, yelling, or grabbing the people involved, he would quickly de-escalate the situation. Because he had the respect of the community and a calm demeanor, he was able to do this multiple times. When he eventually did get a squad car, if someone was too drunk to make it home one night, my grandfather would give them a ride home instead of arresting them for public intoxication. One day, after almost 20 years of service in the department, at the age of 57, my grandfather fell to the floor while relaxing at home. My dad was in college attending FAMU at the time and happened to be at the house. He heard a loud noise hit the floor and ran into the room to see what it was. There he discovered his father on the floor, clutching at his chest. My dad hurried to call 911 for assistance and continued to hold onto his father until they arrived. Sadly, granddad Fred passed away in my dad's arms. The doctors later said that the cause of death was a stroke due to hypertension. Throughout the years, I've wondered if the stress of what he dealt with as a police officer, coupled with holding so much emotion inside, had an impact on his health.

In 2002, the city of Tallahassee honored him with a ceremony where they erected a statue of him in the area of Frenchtown that he used to patrol. His children, which include my dad, my Uncle Freddy, and my late Aunt Gloria, along with several other family members, attended the ceremony. Although he's been gone for many years, his legacy will never be forgotten.

There have been times in my life that I wanted to give up and wanted to make excuses. Many of those times are mentioned throughout this book, but there have been several others. Whenever I've had those thoughts, my mind takes me to different places. As I've gotten older, my faith in God has carried me through many of life's curveballs. Another thing that carries me is thinking about the sacrifices that were made by those that came before me. When I'm frustrated and feel like going off on somebody, I hear my granddaddy Moses', my mother's father, telling me:

"Boy, if you can't say something nice, don't say nothing at all."

I think about how hard he worked to put food on the table for his family, and how with no more than a 5th-grade education he and my grandmother Mary put 7 children through college at FAMU. You'll hear more about my granddaddy Moses in a later chapter. When the pressure is on to meet multiple deadlines at work while also raising a family, working on my marriage, working to build a business, among other things...I think to myself, you don't have it that bad. Think about what granddad Fred went through, and remember his quiet strength. So, when I want to make excuses for anything, I just can't. I owe it to my grandparents, to my parents, to my wife, to my kids, and to all of the people that played a role in raising me to always be on point. Yeah, life gets difficult sometimes, but leaders don't run away when things are hard. So, what inspires you? It's important to know that and to understand the source of it. When you want to give up or make excuses in your life, that inspiration will be the thing to carry you forward.

THREE PILLARS OF ACCOUNTABILITY

RETRAIN YOUR MIND

Earlier in the chapter, we talked about removing the language of excuses from our vocabulary. This sounds easy enough, but how do we actually do it and make it sustainable? As with anything, it will take consistent effort and time. There is a concept that I was recently introduced to that is referred to as mindful awareness practice. At its core, the philosophy is centered on the fact that every human being has the ability to sit in his or her current moment, feel that moment, and redirect his or her response to any situation. A quick scenario to illustrate:

You're on the highway going 70 miles per hour, and another car approaches from behind you going 85, barely misses hitting your car, and jumps in front of you in the lane. In this situation, what is the first emotion you feel? For some, it's anger; they quickly throw up a middle finger and maybe even roll down their window to curse the person out. Another person might be so distraught from the car approaching and almost hitting them that they overcorrect, swerve into another lane to avoid a wreck, and end up hitting another car. Both of these reactions are practically instantaneous because our brain is already trained to respond one-way or the other. Therefore we just react.

Now imagine if you had the ability to control and redirect your brain whenever you wanted. In the scenario above, when you're driving, you look in your rearview mirror and see the car approaching behind you at high speed. Instead of waiting to react, you automatically access the situation and sit in it:

"This car looks like it's approaching way too fast. Let me check the lanes next to me to see if I can carefully switch over."

"Whoever's driving that car is either really in a hurry, completely wreckless, drunk, or all three. Let them pass and get as far away from my car as possible."

This is you sitting in a moment, assessing the situation, and reacting. Not reacting first off of initial emotion, and possibly regretting the outcome of that emotion later. It's a completely different way to approach life situations and daily communication with others. So how is this relevant to making excuses? Because you'll have to do the same thing to ensure excuses are not a trained response that your brain goes to. Throughout the years, I've had countless conversations with friends and associates where the topic was what happened between them and their ex-girlfriend or ex-boyfriend to cause them to break up. Here are two things to listen for whenever someone is talking to you about their ex. It's what I listen for closely:

*"Things didn't work out between us because **I** did _ _ _ _ _"*

*"That relationship and that person **taught me** _ _ _ _ _ _ _ _"*

No excuses or blame, just a person truly sitting at the moment and thinking about what happened while taking personal accountability. Of course, we're excluding relationships where one person has been completely abusive or unhealthy to the other partner; in these cases, the harmed partner needs to realize that they were in a toxic relationship, and the only logical choice was to leave. But for other situations, there is always some level of personal accountability that can be explored. Or what about when you were supposed to turn in your portion of the project at work last week, but you're walking into a meeting to tell the team that you're still not done. As you're headed toward the room, you are already probably thinking about what to say. Someone in the room is going to ask, "So (insert your name), how are things coming with the project?" A very natural reaction is to give all of the reasons that you're late because it is the most natural response. And granted, there may be some very legit reasons for you being late, as we said earlier in the chapter, life happens. But what if when you were asked the question, your response was:

"You know, I realize I was supposed to have that to you last week. That is completely on me. I'm working hard to have all of the details ironed out and will have that to you by the end of the day."

At that point, what is the person going to say? They may not like the fact that you missed your deadline, but they will at least respect the fact that you took accountability for it and didn't blame anything or anyone for it. For the record, one way to avoid this scenario is to over-communicate. If you feel that you're not going to make a deadline, then it is best to let that be known sooner rather than later (reference one of our earlier pillars – bad news doesn't get better with time). The point is to retrain your mind to avoid making excuses a natural response in your personal and professional life. I know this can be done because I've done it and continue to have to work on it. It's a lifelong commitment to change but well worth it.

ALWAYS BE TAKING ACTION

The fear of death is a very real thing for most people. One reason it is scary for most to think about is the unknown nature of it. What comes next after this life? Will I go somewhere, or will I merely cease to exist? Being a Christian, I do believe that another destination exists for me beyond my current reality, and that thought alone brings me a level of peace. Now although I am beginning to spend more time reading and meditating on various bible scriptures, I don't claim to be a bible scholar by any means; nor am I an expert on the afterlife. But I know this, one day, we will all leave this current reality called life for something else. The other thing I know is that none of us know when that is going to happen. Sure, we all picture ourselves living long, full lives well into our 80's and 90's, but many times that is just not how life turns out. If you're reading this, I'm pretty sure you personally knew or have heard of somebody that passed away before the age of 40, or 30, in their 20's or teenage years.

So why did I choose to start off this pillar like this? Because I wanted to drive home the point that none of us have time to waste, not even a single day. We go through life so casually sometimes, assuming that we'll always have tomorrow, next week, next month, or next year to get things done. And although nobody promised us that, we frequently act like it's a guarantee. Is there anything in your life that you want to do so badly that it literally eats you up inside, but for some reason, you haven't taken steps to start? It could be anything because I think that even when we procrastinate on the small things in life, that carries over into the big things. One thing about being a leader is that procrastination is just simply not an option. If you are leading a team, then the team is always watching how you handle situations. When there is a task to get done by a certain deadline, do you rally the team to start taking action, or do you delay having the meeting to talk about it until next week? Now I know what some of you may be thinking. What if I'm simply not ready or don't have all of the answers? If that thought has ever crossed your mind, then it's a completely valid one. It's natural to want to understand 100% about what you're doing and what you're getting into before proceeding forward. However, this mindset of seeking complete understanding through analysis can quickly turn into procrastination.

One of my favorite phrases that I've heard used recently is the power of taking 'imperfect action.' I love that concept because it pretty much sums up what most successful people do. They have a thought, a dream, a concept of some sort...and they act. Of course, they've done the research, studied various facts, and given thought to their plan. But the most important step is action, period. Trust me, I did not write this book for you or anyone else reading it to say, "Wow, what a great read, very solid concepts on leadership. Alright, on to the next book". The entire reason for putting a plan of action at the end of each chapter is to force us to act because nothing else matters. Just imagine how different your life will be after a year of consistently practicing your new leadership plan. You will feel a confidence that you've never felt before, and empathy for people that you may not have realized you had, a determination that was always living inside you and was just dying to get out. But it all starts with making a choice to take action today.

NEVER GIVE UP

I lost close to $30,000 on a rental property investment in 2019, and it really hurt. I bought my first piece of real estate in 2007, and after living in it for a few years, ended up renting it out to a tenant in 2011. After several years of focusing on other business pursuits on the side while working my full-time job, I decided it was time to get serious about expanding my rental portfolio. So, in late 2018 I started looking at buying my next property. After driving through several areas of Dallas, I decided to focus on a few neighborhoods in the Oakcliff area south of downtown. I ended up finding a property and closing on it in March of 2019. Within a month, a property management company had managed to find a tenant to move into the property. I was so excited. The cash flow from this rental would be used to help fund paying down the mortgage even faster on my other rental property until I owned it free and clear. The setup was perfect....

One morning when I was driving to work, I pulled into the parking lot and checked my email. At this point, the new tenants had been in the property for less than a month. There was an email from the property management company stating the following:

"Mr. Lee, there have been several violent incidents reported at your property over the past several weeks. The most recent was a drive-by shooting that ended with a fatality. The tenants are scared and are preparing to move out immediately. Due to this situation, we will, unfortunately, have to terminate our property management contract with you at this time."

I sat in my car for about 10 minutes, completely frozen. I called the property management office, and they described the situation that happened. Apparently, the neighbors said that the people who did the shooting had an issue with someone that lived in the property previously. The day of the shooting, the new tenant's mother was sitting in the car in the driveway when a car pulled up by the home and started shooting from the window. As I sat on the phone, my heart sank. The next 6 months were a complete blur, and I sank into a deep depression. I ended up paying on a mortgage during those 6 months with no income coming in, my air conditioning unit on the side of the house was stolen and had to be replaced, and I had to have several repairs done to the inside and outside of the house due to the bullets that had ricocheted into the home. But much bigger and heavier on my heart than that was the fact that I felt responsible for moving a family into that home. In my mind, if I'd never bought the property, then I wouldn't have hired the property management company that found my tenants. Then they never would have moved there, and their mother would still be alive. I didn't care about any money; the loss of life was the biggest blow. I eventually sold the property in November 2019, despite several people advising me to keep it as an investment. The reality is I couldn't live with the thought of potentially putting anyone else in harm's way; it just wasn't worth it for me. When I signed the closing documents, I knew I'd incurred a huge loss, and I didn't know at the time if I'd ever want anything to do with real estate again.

What have been some of your biggest losses in life? I'm not talking about a time you lost a petty argument with a friend or coworker or anything trivial. I mean, something that rocked your world, was gut wrenching, and you had no idea how you'd make it through. Sit at this moment as you're reading this and remember how you felt. Remember the pain and the heartache of it. Or you might be reading this and are experiencing a loss like that right now. Truthfully, in this life everyone takes losses, including leaders. When you dare to lead, that means that you dare to take risks, and when you take risks, you will undoubtedly lose sometimes. And guess

what, that's ok. This pillar's plan of action will be one of the more important ones in this book, so please practice it in your life. I don't know what
you're going through right now, what you've overcome in the past, or what
you might have to deal with in the future. Regardless of what it is, I want
to encourage you to remember that there are no losses in life, only lessons.
So continue to press forward, be bold, be daring, take risks and pursue
your dreams. Believe me, this section is for me just as much as it's for you,
so let's keep pressing forward together.

What Introverts Wish Extroverts knew

When it comes to accountability and ownership, we can make a great team.
If we have a goal that we're working to meet, remember that I'm extremely
detailed. So I will know exactly where it is that we're trying to go and the
steps that it takes to get there. If we have a setback, circumstances cause
us to lose momentum, or we have just veered off course from our goal due
to a lack of focus, then I will help us to get back on track. Because I know
and spend so much time focusing on the detailed plan, I am a great person
to help hold the team accountable.

Plan of Action

Retrain your mind – This tip is all about changing our language. Start
listening to your friends, family members, co-workers, and others when
they're speaking and listen closely for excuses. As you actively listen for it,
you'll start to recognize it. Concurrently, do the same thing for yourself.
Make a conscious effort to take accountability if you've done something
wrong, and start paying attention to your words before you say them.

It may take time, continue this until you notice your overall language has changed.

Always be taking action – Write down something that you want to get done. This may be one major thing, or it may be a 'to do' list with multiple things on it. Regardless, write down what you have to do, and take at least one action toward that list today. It doesn't matter if the action is large or small, do it today. **No seriously.... today!** Ok, I think you get the point.

Never Give Up – Write down the biggest personal, professional, or financial loss you've taken in your life. If you need to write down more than one, that is ok. Now I want you to write all of the lessons that you learned from the experience. Here are a few personal lessons that I learned from the rental property story I told in this chapter:

- Never invest without guidance from a mentor.
- Always research and understand crime statistics for any area where you're looking to purchase the property.
- Always budget adequately for tenant vacancy and for repairs when buying real estate.
- Never make a significant life decision without involving God and my wife.

Those were the lessons for me. I hope that as you put your list together, you will learn and grow stronger from it. As I said, we're in this together.

CHAPTER 5 – HUMILITY

"Success is on the team; failure is on me"
Chris Byrd, Project Engineer (my former mentor)

What makes people follow a leader? In some cases, a person has been promoted to a leadership position at the company they work for, or they assume the role in their business, and they're really just a manager. A manager can tell people what they're supposed to do and point people to the resources they'll need to get their job done. A leader can inspire people, build trust, show empathy, and is genuinely invested in growing other leaders. So, managers and leaders are vastly different. The best teams build a culture that is focused on winning and accomplishing the ultimate goal for the larger group.

If you think about it, any high-performing team that performs well more often than not, has a strong leader or a group of leaders in place. A child's parents, or parent, are the leaders of their home. That child's future will likely be a direct reflection of the strength or weakness of leadership that they experience in the home. A teacher is a leader to a classroom full of students. A business owner is a leader for his or her employees. A project lead is a leader for his or her peers at work. In all of these cases, the leader desires to be effective at helping others to achieve a goal and wants everyone on the team to perform at their highest potential. At the same time, the person or people who are being led desire to have an effective leader. So how do both the leader and the one being led achieve their objectives? In the end, there are two character-traits that the leader must possess that will make or break his or her team. Every leader must have a healthy balance of confidence and humility. This balance makes it easy to practice an extremely important action that many leaders never truly understand. I have seen the action fumbled and mishandled on several programs that I've worked on throughout my career. Conversely, I've seen the action handled by leaders correctly and witnessed the benefit of it. The action can be summed up in one word: ownership.

My favorite leadership book of all time is Extreme Ownership by Jocko Willink and Leif Babin. I read this book in 2017. At the time, I was a project engineer responsible for technical leadership of a full-rate production aircraft program at a Fortune 500 defense contractor. Extreme Ownership literally changed my view of what it meant to be a leader. You see, before reading that book, I assumed that whenever things went well, the leader should get most of the credit. After all, they're the ones with the big title, whose name appears on the organizational charts, and everyone knows them. When things went horribly wrong, and there was no place to turn, it wasn't the leader's fault...right? In any team situation, there are usually several people with various responsibilities and assignments, which leads to several potential points of failure. I used to believe that in the majority of team scenarios, any plan that failed could be attributed to the actions of one or more other individuals on the team.

Well, the extreme ownership philosophy debunks that completely. To summarize the key takeaway, essentially **anything** that occurs on a team, good or bad, comes down to the effectiveness of the leader. So, what does this mean? If you're leading a team of 4 students for a group project at school and the project gets turned in a week late, whose fault is that? If you're leading a team at work, your team owes a finished product to the customer by tomorrow, and your team doesn't make the deadline, who does that fall on? The answer in both of these cases is that it falls on the leader. Self-reflection is hard, taking responsibility is hard, but these are the personality traits of a true leader. If your team's group project at school got turned in late, did you set reasonable expectations upfront for everyone on the team? Did everyone understand their roles and responsibilities clearly? If not, then you have no one to blame but yourself. If your team at work didn't meet the customer deadline, did you identify potential risks that could impact your team's ability to meet that date upfront and actively work to mitigate those risks along the way? It's a complete shift in thinking for most people; I know it was for me. But you're a leader, so you no longer get to think any other way. From now on, if you're reading this... realize that if you plan to grow into a leader, it is not always filled with praise and perfection. When mistakes are made, it's on you as the leader to act with humility, take responsibility for what happened, and own it.

THE ABSENT BROTHER, THE ABSENT SON

My sister and I grew up really close. When I was around 5 years old, I used to beg my mom and dad for a brother, a sister, a dog, anyone, or anything to keep me company. I wanted a playmate, somebody to hang out with. So, in September of 1987, my sister Valerie was born in San Francisco, California; I was 6 at the time. I instantly loved being a big brother; I felt like it was my responsibility to watch out for my little sister, and I took it seriously. In most brother and sister relationships, there's typically a level of sibling rivalry that exists. Name calling, teasing, and annoying each other, among other things, are common. I know this because my wife and I watch our two toddlers do it from time to time right now. I can honestly say that Valerie and I didn't have much of that. There's a videotape of her 3rd birthday when she was getting gifts and money from a number of our relatives, and I was upset because I wasn't getting any. Every time my parents would hand her a gift or a card with money in it, I would roll my eyes and frown my face up. It's actually a pretty hilarious video (and no, it will never be shown in public). That is probably the closest I can ever remember being anywhere near upset with my sister, and even then, I wasn't upset with her; it was the situation.

We grew up playing basketball, watching shows on Nickelodeon like 'Are You Afraid of the Dark', which for some reason terrified us at the time, and had our family pet, a hamster which my sister affectionately called Ginger MC Hammer Precious Lee (it was the 90's). When we lived in Rochester, on days when school would be closed due to a snowstorm hitting the area the night before, we would go outside covered in three layers of clothing, and ride our plastic sleds down the hill in the backyard together. As our family moved around to different cities and the years passed, I started to develop more relationships with new friends, especially when I got to high school. In what seemed like the blink of an eye, I looked up, and it was time to graduate and move on to college. I packed up my things, loaded up my Toyota Camry with my parents and my sister, and we started heading to Tallahassee, Florida.

We had a family get-together on the last night before my parents and my sister were going to be leaving to drive back to Dallas. We had several family members living in Tallahassee that were there to welcome me to the city. When most college students are getting dropped off at school for their freshmen year, they can't wait to say goodbye. This is college, which means freedom! But not me; that's not what I felt that night. As I was sitting there at the family function while everyone else was talking and having a good time, I started to feel sad, really sad. Then it happened. It was finally time for my parents and my sister to go. Valerie and I gave each other a big hug and wouldn't let go. She started crying, and I was trying to hold back tears, trying to hold up to the standard I'd always believed that men didn't cry. I remember one of our cousins saying, "Wow, me and my brother ain't nothing like that. You all actually love each other, huh?". Eventually, my parents and Valerie got in the car. Valerie looked out of the back window of the car and started waving at me as the car began to pull away. I still remember waving back at her and watching as the car drove off. Then I started to cry uncontrollably, I don't know what took over me, but I couldn't hold it in anymore. Despite how excited I was to start my next chapter in life, I realized at that moment how much I really did love my dad, my mom, and my sister.

As the years began to pass while I was in college, I would typically come back to Dallas during the winter break and the summers. When I would be back home, my sister and my parents would want to hang out; during the semesters when I was in Tallahassee, we would talk on the phone, but several months would go by without us seeing each other. Instead of spending a lot of time with my family while in Dallas, I chose to spend a lot of my time catching up with my friends from high school. It was common for there to be nights when we'd be at my parent's house, Valerie, my mom, and dad would have somewhere they wanted us to go as a family, or they would want to all watch a Dallas Mavericks game together. Instead of planning to stay there with them, I would already have plans to go out with my friends. The Mavericks game would start right around the time I was getting ready to head out of the door to meet my friends somewhere. I would wave goodbye as my parents, and my sister sat on the couch in the living room. I did this consistently as the years went on; even when I graduated from FAMU in fall of 2004 and came home to Dallas, the trend was the same. It's not that we never spent time together as a family at all, and I enjoyed being with my friends, so it's not that I regret the time spent with them. The issue was that I consistently prioritized time with my friends over my family; I rarely found myself prioritizing my family over my friends.

This was the same family that had believed in me, supported me, that had loved me despite all of my flaws and my mistakes over the years. When I would mess up in school or at home, somehow my mom would always find a way to defend me despite my wrongs and give me encouragement. When I was dating and would have a relationship go south, my mom and my sister had my back every time, even sometimes when I might not have deserved it. When I went through some of the hardest times in my life, like losing my scholarship in college, multiple breakups, and a number of others, I knew that I could talk to my sister. She would always find a way to make me feel better, to make me believe in myself again. When I got a flat tire on the extremely busy interstate 183 highway in Dallas, as I sat in my car on the shoulder with other cars passing within a few feet of me at over 80 miles per hour, the first person I called was my dad. He came to meet me as soon as I called him. He led me to a safe location away from the highway and then proceeded to help me fix the flat tire. Ironically my friends that I was spending so much time with didn't cross my mind to call anytime that I ended up in a situation like that. It was always my dad; the flat tire situation was just one time among many. Regardless of what was going on in my life, I knew he would always answer, and he would always be there for me. I had no idea how my not spending time with the family was affecting them until having a conversation with my sister one day. She opened my eyes to a lot of things that I had completely ignored and hadn't thought about. I remember feeling humbled, ashamed, and disappointed in myself for not putting the people first that always had my back.

These days my sister and her husband have two kids, and my wife and I have two kids. My parents are now grandparents with four grandchildren, and I know they love the experience. I oftentimes reflect on how selfish I was in my college years and in my 20's and how many moments I missed with my sister and my parents. I realize that I can't get those moments back, so I had to take ownership and accept that those missed moments are on me. These days I enjoy going to my parent's house with my family and spending quality, unhurried time together. My sister and her family live in Houston, so whenever they are in Dallas, or we're in Houston, I purposely don't make plans for anything else or with anyone else during that time. The time with my family today means so much to me that it's hard to put into words; I just try to be present in all of the moments that we have together. I own that I wasn't always there as a brother for Val or as a son for my mom and dad, so for the rest of my life, I hope to be.

THREE PILLARS OF
HUMILITY

CELEBRATE SMALL WINS

It's common for people to set big goals for themselves. When I was in college majoring in engineering, there were several challenging courses that I put a number of hours into. Neural Networks, Thermodynamics, and Advanced Electronic Circuits are a few that come to mind. I used to set goals for the grades that I wanted to get at the end of each semester. I would write out the 4 to 5 classes that I was scheduled to take, and next to each one, I would write down the grade that I hoped to get. The semester would start, and all that was on my mind was getting the particular grade that I wanted at the end. I would hand in homework assignments, take quizzes and exams, with the ultimate goal being to end up with that grade or better. Now in some of these classes, I was able to meet my goal, while others I wasn't. Ultimately, I wish I had set my focus on small wins instead of just the big picture. For example, there were some extremely difficult tests that I got A's on when the majority of the class got a lower grade. Or when I'd expected to get a low B or a C on the test. In cases like that, I should have taken time to stop and celebrate that win. I was too worried about ending up where I needed to be in the end to take the moment in and appreciate it.

It is critical to your morale to recognize and acknowledge when things are going right. Just as attention is put on issues and problems that you and your team might face, the same attention needs to be put on wins. When I was in my network marketing business, one of the things that we did was make a big deal anytime someone on our team signed up a new business partner. The business was structured where you had to sign up a certain number of people in order to qualify for the company's residual income and bonus payouts. But even if someone hadn't signed up a single person, when they brought their first business partner on board, we made a huge deal out of it. This was the type of morale boost that people needed, and it made a difference. Part of having humility is appreciating the accomplishments of other people. Don't wait for some major milestone or achievement to be the first time you say thank you to someone on your team. This becomes increasingly difficult in environments that are busy and have aggressive deadlines. Everybody is heads down working on their particular tasks for the day, so nobody is thinking about the progress being made. Days, weeks, and months might go by without anybody on a team hearing a single thank you or being congratulated for the work they've done. In many cases, this is not being done maliciously; again it can just become the unfortunate byproduct of a team that is too busy.

In reality, thanking and appreciating others should be a part of the daily culture of the teams that you lead. Remember, teams take on the personality of the leader. So, if the leader is in a constant state of being thankful for the team's wins, and the leader is remaining humble, then others will be that way too. A simple thank you probably doesn't sound like much, but it goes a long way.

GIVE YOUR TEAMMATES THE CREDIT

When people are giving acceptance speeches for awards or are being acknowledged by their peers for doing a good job at something, I like to pay attention to what they say. The way that a person reacts to praise tells you a lot about them. It's easy to get caught up in our own hype, to believe that when we accomplish amazing things in life, it was solely due to our abilities and our intellect. But to date, I have yet to meet a successful individual that got to their position in life on their own. Real leaders recognize this, which is why you'll often hear them shout out their team whenever they experience a win. All of the great leaders that I've encountered in my life have done this, and I've made it a point to do the same myself whenever possible.

Let's say you are a project lead for a multi-million-dollar contract at your company, with a team of over 30 people that are performing various roles on the project. The project spans over 1 year, and at the end of that year, there will be a product delivered to the customer. During that year, you and the team work extremely hard, sometimes putting in over 60 hours a week at the office, going through struggles, and solving countless issues that come up. Throughout this time, you are the primary interface to the customer whenever they want a status of how the project is going. There is a weekly tag-up meeting that you lead with the customer where you provide updates. Toward the end of the project, things are starting to fall behind, so you and the team now have to work twice as hard to meet the deadline that you've promised. In the end, you and the team end up delivering the product on time, literally on the day that it was scheduled to be ready in your contract. It is a huge accomplishment, and the customer calls a meeting where your entire team is invited. The customer starts off the meeting by thanking you by name for your leadership during the project and says that the project couldn't have happened without you. You're then given an award, and everyone starts to applaud. Now don't get me wrong, positive affirmation and receiving praise feels good. It actually feels great! My wife and I took a test to find out our love languages, and the top one for me is words of affirmation. So I enjoy getting positive reinforcement from others. At the same time though, a leader has to be very careful about not letting praise and affirmation get to their head. There is a team that has been working hard just like you, putting in long hours just like you, and making sacrifices just like you. If you want to build an unbreakable trust and loyalty with your team, give the credit for all wins to them.

So in the scenario where now you're standing in front of the room, or you're preparing to speak on a call after receiving thunderous applause, it's time to lift up your team. Don't talk about yourself. Talk about them. One thing to note here, be very careful about calling out names specifically. If it is a smaller team (3-5 people), then you'll probably have an easier time speaking to the contributions of each person involved. However, if the team is a larger one, then it is oftentimes best to give credit to the team as a whole, speak to the challenges that they overcame and the outstanding job they did to get the project to this point. When you start to give credit by name, then you run the risk of missing somebody; I have actually made this mistake myself.

Example: one teammate (we'll call him Joe) didn't hear his name mentioned during your speech where you shouted out over 20 other people. Joe has worked a double shift for the past 2 weeks, and as a result of that, he hasn't been spending a lot of time with his family. He also has been 100% on board with the project and with this team because he believes in the product being delivered. How do you think Joe feels now that credit is being given to everyone on the team, but he doesn't hear his name? Joe's morale is now shot. He starts to feel invisible and unnoticed, eventually Joe decides to start looking for a position on another team, and ends up leaving.

This is just an example of what can happen. Now, if there is something that a person on the team did that they were solely responsible for that's different, call them out by name and give them their credit in front of the team. This is a huge morale boost for them and will make them feel appreciated. But for large team wins, make sure the credit is given to all involved.

In my opinion, a leader should always be thinking team first, me second. This attitude not only keeps the leader humble but it makes it easy to praise others and give them credit when it's due. When your team feels recognized and knows they are seen, you will build a culture of people that want you as their leader.

SHIELD YOUR TEAM

I love an analogy that my pastor used one Sunday during his sermon. Pastor Conway Edwards at the One Community Church where I attend was preaching about 'running the play'. With running the play being a metaphor for how Christians can reach people and deliver the gospel of Jesus in today's world where so much has changed. Carrying a football in his hand, he talked about how some people try to run a play by them-selves. While people are trying to tackle them, bring them to the ground, and strip them of the ball, they continue with no protection. However, if there's an offensive lineman in front of that person (in this analogy, the lineman represents God), now they are protected and have someone blocking for them on their way to score. Now I recognize you might be reading this book and not be a Christian or not religious at all for that matter. If that's the case, then it's all good. I respect you and am with you no matter what your belief system is, so this analogy can be helpful for you regardless. A leader should be the one that shields their team from any negativity, any distractions, and any trouble whenever possible.

If a customer is upset that their order is late, it doesn't matter if the reason is that Bob has been showing up late to work this week, so the project hasn't been getting worked on. It doesn't matter if someone on the team forgot to email a copy of the latest presentation to you prior to your meeting with the leadership team. As a leader, when you get asked the inevitable ques-tion, "What happened?" your response is never to blame people on your team. Your response and verbiage need to indicate to everyone that you are, in fact, a team. So instead of:

"Well, customer, Bob didn't get to put much time on the task this week, so we're running a little behind. I'm getting with him today to make sure he steps it up."

It should be

*"Well, customer, **we** really need to get more time put into the project this week. It has turned out to be greater scope than **we** originally considered, so **we** are actively allocating the right resources to get it done.*

You see the difference? Now behind closed doors away from anyone else, you need to be sure and have a candid discussion with your team about their performance. What you don't want is to enable bad behavior because if a person isn't told when they're messing up, then they won't know. The key is to not do this publicly in front of the team, in front of customers, or others in general. Again, the leader is the one that has signed up to take the blame and to shield the team whenever things aren't going well. This mentality can also not be achieved without humility because it requires you to truly be unselfish. Remember this phrase that my old mentor Chris Byrd used to always tell me "Success is on the team; Failure is on me."

What Introverts Wish Extroverts knew

There are a variety of introvert personality types, some with a wide range of meanings from one to the other; but there is one trait that is typically common among most introverts. That trait is the ability to show empathy for other people. With me on your team, you will have someone that likely has, or has the potential to have, a high emotional intelligence when dealing with others. This is extremely important in any work environment or business where interactions with people can make or break a team's success (which is almost every industry to a degree). Because I tend to show empathy for others, and I usually don't crave the spotlight, it allows me to stay humble and to be someone that you will love to work with.

Plan of Action

Celebrate small wins – If you are currently in a leadership position or a part of a team, write down something that recently went well for your team. It doesn't matter how big or how small the accomplishment was, have you or anyone on the team recognized it yet? If there are several things that should be recognized, then that's great; write all of them down on a list. Recognition for these things could come in the form of an award being given to someone or even a simple thank you. Take the initiative and make sure that anyone that was a part of the effort feels appreciated and feels seen. The main takeaway here is that if you identify something that deserves to be recognized, then do your part to ensure that happens.

Give your teammates credit – The next time you are being recognized for a job well done on your team, begin to make it a practice to talk about what other people did to help you. I suggest already having a list in mind of people that are currently helping you with whatever project you are currently working on. Now I realize this is hard, we're human, and a large majority of us enjoy affirmation, recognition, and attention. But start to make it a practice for your first thought to be about who you can pass the praise to, instead of accepting all of the praise yourself. Begin to try this in your personal life with your friends, family, or significant other as well. That will help you with getting used to it as a new way of thinking.

Shield your team – If you're currently a leader, be careful with your language when communicating any bad news. Use "we" instead of calling out names when describing specific problems. If you're not currently in a leadership role, make it a habit to observe how leaders around you deliver bad news. What type of language do they use? Do they tend to blame others, or do they take ownership and assume responsibility? You will learn a lot about the type of leader that you want to be or the type of leader that you don't from interactions like these. The focus here is to start using "we" language, and anytime you see someone on your team being talked about by somebody in a negative way or blamed for something, you stand up for them. Not only that, but you step up and take the blame for what went wrong in their place. This is humility; this is true leadership.

CHAPTER 6
– AUTHENTICITY

"If you focus instead on being your authentic self and being comfortable with whatever comes with that, then it will truly change your life, and you will be able to lead."

You may be familiar with the analogy of wearing the mask, meaning when a person hides their true feelings or their true selves from other people. The late Paul Laurence Dunbar's poem titled 'We Wear the Mask' says:

We wear the mask that grins and lies,

It hides our cheeks and shades our eyes,

This debt we pay to human guile;

With torn and bleeding hearts, we smile,

And mouth with myriad subtleties.

As human beings, we long to be accepted by others; it's a natural thing. We want people to feel like we're doing well in life, to feel like we have it all together. When we post on social media, we want everyone to see the latest vacation we took out of the country, the new relationship we've gotten into, our new car, our new house, newly born baby. We want people to see all of our wins. We then want to see as many people as possible like and comment on our pictures and our videos. So why is that? I believe that much of it is all connected to our strong desire to be accepted. Take the scenario when we're at a dinner party with friends and everyone is talking about their latest accomplishments, their new house, new job, new everything. In that situation some of us sit there, listen and contribute to the conversation when we feel compelled to do so. While others of us hear the stories of success being shared around the table, and immediately begin to compare ourselves, questioning why we haven't achieved what everyone else there has. In the past, I have absolutely been in rooms and thought this. And since we're being honest here, I've brought up things in conversations with groups of people in the past about my career, business pursuits, and other things simply because I wanted to give off the impression that I was keeping up with everybody else's success. I would measure how my life was going based on how I would see or hear another person's life was progressing. Even if I was going through a difficult time financially or in my personal life, you would never know it. Anyone talking to me would leave the conversation feeling like Terrance was on top of things.

Part of building solid team dynamics, and part of being an exceptional leader, is the ability to be authentic. Two common synonyms for the word authentic are genuine and real. If you're going to lead teams, then it's extremely important that your team sees your authentic and true self at all times. This means speaking up against things that you feel are wrong, it means not compromising your character or your core belief system to appease other people, it means not being worried about always fitting in, and it means that you have to be ok with the reality that you won't always make everybody happy. Lastly, it means that if you are reading this and your personality is introverted, you should not be trying to act like an extrovert. I'll say that one more time; do not try to act like an extrovert if you're not one! We'll talk more about that here shortly.

Let's face it, we can tell when someone is being fake, and we can typically tell when someone is just telling us what we want to hear. This is not the culture that you want to build for your team. When people feel like they have to suppress their true personalities and their true feelings, you have basically created a wall. That wall will prevent open and honest communication, which is essential for your team to win. Imagine you have an employee that has recently lost a loved one, and you have no idea. If they feel that the team's culture is one where they could share that information and receive support, now they begin to view that team as a family. However, if the culture is one where people keep their private business to themselves and essentially "wear the mask" despite any difficulties that happen, then that employee will most likely keep the news of the recent loss to themself. Or maybe as a leader, you are overworked and are tired; trust me, I know because I have been there! Do you continue to operate this way? A better approach is to be open and honest with your team and communicate that you need help. This has a positive impact for a few reasons:

- It shows your team that you are humble enough to ask for help, that humility will be noticed and admired.
- It gives someone else on the team an opportunity to gain valuable experience through helping with some of your work. That can end up being valuable for their career growth.

When leaders and their teams are communicating in an authentic way, then great things can happen. I've seen situations where the leaders of an organization have created a culture where people were afraid to speak their mind if their thought disagreed in any way with the leader's. I've also seen cultures where everybody on the team felt empowered, and nobody's voice was valued above anyone else's. Those are by far the best environments to work in and are typically the most productive. It took me a long time to be comfortable with being my authentic self. I used to worry about what people would think about me, I would worry about offending the wrong person if I spoke my opinion, and I used to worry about if I would be accepted. My mentality today is completely different, and I can say that I've felt the shift in my leadership style as a result. Ultimately, you can't live your life wearing a mask to hide the truth, dying for acceptance, and hoping to please everybody. If so, you'll fall short every time. If you focus instead on being your authentic self and being comfortable with whatever comes with that, then it will truly change your life, and you will be able to lead.

DAD – THE STANDARD

From the time I was a little boy, I longed for my dad's approval. Growing up in a Christian household, my parents and our extended family were always very religious. My family went to church every Sunday; there had to be something seriously wrong for us to miss a week. We were typically one of the first families to get to the church and one of the last families to leave. Mainly because my mom, an extreme extrovert that loves people, would not leave until she had spoken to every person in the church lobby first. My dad served as a deacon and eventually an elder at our church in North Dallas and held positions in other churches prior to that, while my mother was director for several church choirs. Education was also held in high regard in our house, and performing well in school was an expectation. So, if there was anything that I wanted growing up, it was for my dad to think that I had my spiritual life together and was doing well in school.

My parents grew up in Tallahassee, Florida, home to Florida A&M University where I went to college, Florida State University and the state capitol. My dad arrived at Rickards High School as a freshman; at a time when schools in Leon County were first being integrated. Going into his senior year of high school, he was trying to figure out the next steps for his life. Around that time, the dean of the business school at FAMU was Dr. Sybill Mobley. Due to him being one of the highest performers in his class Dr. Mobley offered him an accounting scholarship to attend FAMU, he actually didn't even know what accounting was at the time. However, he decided to attend FAMU, only a few miles away from the home he grew up in.

While attending school, he did extremely well and ended up graduating second in his class. Upon graduation, he received a job offer from Coopers and Liebrant as an accountant. After working for a few years, he was given his first leadership role as a senior accountant auditor, where he would regularly work 60 to 80 hour weeks. He attended his first leadership program while working at General Electrical in Peakskill, New York. This program opened his eyes to leadership principles and philosophies for the first time in his life. He would later get an opportunity as a general accounting manager in Dallas. His career continued to progress, to the point where he eventually became a Chief Financial Officer (CFO) at a firm in Dallas where he worked for several years.

I never knew many details about what he did growing up, all I knew was that my dad was an accountant, was very smart, was good at what he did, and he worked extremely hard at it. Anything that I saw my dad do, he always put his all into it, and it was obvious that people respected him for that. So this became the bar that I measured myself against professionally. From a spiritual standpoint, my dad was revered for his wisdom and dedication to his faith. Here was a man that at my parent's 40th wedding anniversary party, one friend of his called him "the holiest man that I know." It was common growing up to see my dad be the one that everyone would ask to lead prayer at the dinner table in their homes, or the one that people at the church would ask to mentor their children if they were going through a tough time. A man that had a successful career. A man that had the ultimate love and respect of his family, friends, and colleagues. He was who I wanted to be and who I wanted so badly to impress.

Around the age of 14 is when I started to live a double life. It started small, listening to my cassette tapes where I'd recorded my favorite rap songs from the radio on my walkman. For anyone reading this that might be younger than me, and has no idea what a walkman is, it's a device we used way back in the day to play music. This was many years before streaming platforms existing! Anyway, when my dad came around, I would quickly stop the music, afraid of what he'd say if he heard what I was listening to. As soon as he would walk away, I would slowly turn up the volume of Notorious BIG, Nas, Ice Cube, Outkast, or others in my headphones. Later in the ninth grade, when I was now a freshman that was interested in girls and had friends that were telling their stories about the first time they had sex, I wouldn't dare ask my parents for their thoughts on that topic. The church answer that Christian folks say regarding sex is quick and simple, and anyone that grew up in a household like mine can probably guess what I'm going to say: no sex until you get married, period, end of discussion. Eventually, when I got to high school, I was in Sunday school every week, going to church retreats and even helping my dad some weeks in the audio booth working the sound during our church service. But many mornings at church, I had just been out the night before with my friends drinking beer, or hanging out at a house party that my parents knew nothing about. That next morning, prior to leaving my room, I would brush my teeth twice and gargle with listerine in hopes that there wouldn't be any hint of alcohol on my breath.

It got to a point where it became a normal routine; my biggest fear was being a disappointment to my parents, so I just continued to hide everything that I was doing. This continued into college when I left Dallas for school in Tallahassee. I remember getting phone calls from my dad on several Sunday afternoons where he would ask, "So son, did you make it to church today?" After a long night of partying, my answer was typically no. When I did go, he would ask me what the sermon was about, to which I usually gave a very vague response. Besides feeling like I didn't measure up to the spiritual standard while in college, I ran into academic issues at times as well. Needless to say, the two areas where I longed to make my dad proud the most, having my spiritual life together and doing well academically, were areas that I constantly felt like a failure.

One day at the age of 38, now a man with a wife and two kids, I got to have a very honest and open conversation with my dad. The details of that talk are not for this book because that is between me, him, and God. But it was honestly what I feel like I'd always needed from him. One of the things that I love about our relationship these days is that I feel free to be myself around him. On Father's Day in 2019, we went to a place called Top Golf together on a Sunday afternoon and got to play golf for a few hours. A defining moment happened when the waitress came to our area, and I ordered a beer in front of him. Now what's interesting is that I don't drink anywhere near as often or as much as I did in college, or when I was an event promoter in my 20's. But I do still enjoy some occasional beers when watching a game or relaxing at home. Prior to the conversation with my dad, I would have never even looked at alcohol in front of him. But now, here I was, feeling comfortable to be myself. Some of you might be out there thinking; what's the big deal, it's just a beer. It really wasn't about the beer; that wasn't the point. It was that I was beginning to feel authentic. The masks were finally gone. Although our relationship will always be father and son, I take comfort in knowing that I can also now call my dad my friend. Our conversations feel authentic and real now because we're free to be open with each other, and there is no judgment.

Ironically, I find myself becoming more like him as the years pass, and my mindset has been changing. I say phrases all the time to my 5 and 3-year old children that my dad used to say to me without even realizing it. Most importantly, the years of going to church, him reading bible scriptures to me, and having conversations with me about how he grew in his faith had an impact. Today I find myself teaching bible verses to my children, looking forward to praying, reading the bible regularly, listening to gospel music, and a number of other things that I would have never thought I'd be doing consistently. What's best is that none of it is forced or meant to impress other people; it's just starting to become a part of who I am. At the same time, the reality is that I still enjoy things that might cause some hardcore religious people to question me. I enjoy hip-hop music, enjoy movies from the '90s, enjoy a cold beer in front of a football game, and enjoy occasional happy hours with friends. Ultimately, I've found comfort in the fact that my focus is no longer on worrying about what other people might think about me. Instead, I choose to be me, and to just focus on growing and improving everyday. For me, the pursuit of working to live my life in the way that Jesus Christ did, despite my many mistakes, continues to transform me and continues to put me at peace.

I may never be the man that my dad is, he has set the bar incredibly high, and I've got a long way to go. I'm forever grateful to him and my mom for the foundation they've given me because I wouldn't be here without it. My hope now is simply that I will always strive to be my best authentic self and to use the gifts that I've been blessed with as long as I'm able to do so.

Fake Excited

"Terrance, I like your presentation. As far as delivering the facts and the information, you do a great job. The only problem is... well, I'm just going to say it, it was a little boring. Need to add a lot more energy to it."

These were the words of my upline business partner Kurt Anderson in one of the network marketing companies that I joined in my early 30's. At the time, me and the other National Directors (a leadership position in the company) were practicing our presentations of the business for him to offer his suggestions and critique. Out of all of the National Directors on our team, I was the one that got the boring label when I spoke. I'll admit that when I heard it, I was bothered by it. I wasn't upset with him at all for saying it; in fact, I had a lot of respect for him and still do today when I look back on the time we were in business together. I think it bothered me because for the first time, I asked myself the following question:

How will I ever be successful if I can't be exciting like everyone else?

I spent a lot of time thinking about that question. Add to that the fact that almost everyone I was spending time with at that point in my life, with the exception of my then fiancé, was an extrovert. The other National Directors were outgoing, social, and when they spoke in front of crowds, they did so with excitement and passion. And the reality is that excitement and passion were central to our business model. In network marketing, one of the keys is to be able to paint a picture for someone. That picture will typically either be you showing them how they can save money or showing them how they can make money. For either one of those, many people seem to feed off of high-energy interaction. We used to have weekly private business receptions where guests were invited to hear about our business opportunity at a ballroom in a hotel. The presentations were always done by someone that was high energy and extremely extroverted. They would engage with the crowd, inserting jokes that would draw laughs, painting pictures of how the person sitting there would be able to quit their 9 to 5 job with this opportunity. One of the major selling points was near the end of the presentation, where the presenter would show everyone a picture of the BMW they would be given if they reached the level of Senior Vice President, and the Bentley they would be given at the Platinum Senior Vice President level. This would usually draw some level of emotion from the crowd as they began to see themselves standing next to their new vehicle. Typically, there was always at least one person that would sign up to join the business that night. Usually it was many more than that.

I had joined the business under my friend Mike, the same Mike that I was an event promoter with, and we took it extremely seriously. Every day we were either contacting prospects, contacting people on our team, leading conference calls, attending business meetings, or a number of other activities for the business. Mike was able to build a strong organization and earned the nickname "Money Mike." He's a dynamic speaker and has a lot of energy, so people were naturally drawn to him. I also was able to build a team that I was now leading in the business, which felt great considering I didn't sign up anybody in my first network marketing experience. But my approach was very different. I preferred to present to people in smaller settings. Business partners in my downline would typically invite me to do business receptions for people at their homes, sometimes 3 or at most 10 people. In those environments, I would usually do well, but I still didn't present with the level of energy that any of the other National Directors had. Whenever our entire team would come together as a group, I would usually find myself fading to the background, as everyone else tended to dominate the conversations.

So, one day I decided to try something. I said to myself, the next time I present, I'm going to be exciting. Now I didn't know exactly what that meant at the time. I just knew that my goal was to not be boring. To be exciting and lively like everyone else in the business was. So, I started doing it. I would raise my voice level frequently, was more animated with my hands, added more jokes to my presentation, and more facial expressions. I was convinced that this was exactly what my business had been missing; I would now start to sign up new partners left and right. Well, after doing this for a few weeks, I noticed that my business was essentially growing at the same pace that it had been before. In addition to that, for some reason, I started to feel drained, I didn't know what it was, but the business began to feel like a burden, something that I didn't look forward to anymore.

In hindsight, I lost interest in the business because I felt like I had lost myself. I was trying so hard to be something that I wasn't, pretending to take on a new persona, thinking that it was the answer. So I'm grateful for the many lessons about leadership and financial freedom that I learned during my time in the network marketing industry. But one major lesson that I learned is that regardless of the situation, if I'm not able to be my authentic self, then I just can't do it. So, I'm reminded of the question that I asked myself back in 2012:

How will I ever be successful if I can't be exciting like everyone else?

Earlier in the book, we spoke about the success of introverts like Shonda Rhimes, Warren Buffet, JK Rowlings, and Barack Obama. But there are so many others, Mark Zuckerberg, Steven Spielberg, Michael Jordan, and Elon Musk, just to name a few. Ultimately introversion does not mean that one cannot stand out, cannot be seen or heard. I had to learn that one of the most important keys to success is truly embracing who you are.

THREE PILLARS OF AUTHENTICITY

NEVER COMPARE YOURSELF TO ANYONE

Have you ever been having a great day; you know, those days when everything seems to be going right, and life is just flowing? Then you start watching a show on television, look at your social media feed or talk to a friend. On TV, you see a group of successful people and think to yourself:

"It sure would be nice to be a millionaire and live like that."

On social media, you see pictures posted by someone you follow and think:

"Wow, I wish I was going on a vacation like that soon."

Then your friend talks about the new house they plan to buy, and you think:

"I'm really happy for them, maybe one day I'll be able to purchase a house in that price range."

Next thing you know, your mind starts wandering down a rabbit hole, you create an alternate reality where you have those things, and you picture a life full of happiness and no worries. Have you ever done this? It's an easy thing to do, and oftentimes, we don't even realize it's happening. Next thing we know, we're subconsciously walking around with something to prove, with some standard that we feel we need to live up to. Because after all, we've been consumed with watching people that appear (keyword – appear) to have it all together. This quickly leads us down a dangerous path that has no end. When we're trying to be someone that we're not, it just never works, and in the end, the people around us can see right through it. So instead of being concerned with what everyone else is doing and what everyone else has accomplished, we should focus on what we know and what we can control. When a leader is operating as their true self, people see it and respect it.

I will say that I have been around some amazing speakers in both my professional career and in various business ventures. In 2012 I attended a business conference in Las Vegas for the network marketing company that I just spoke about in this chapter, and I remember hearing a number of impactful speakers back to back one Saturday afternoon. I literally left the conference feeling like superman; talk about motivation! I was ready to sell products to anyone with a pulse after those speeches. A few business partners and I caught a taxi when we left the convention center that day; I sat in the front seat and spent the entire ride talking to the cab driver about the products in our business. When we arrived at our stop, he took my business card. We all left the taxi and headed to the hotel lobby, where we spent the next few hours calling potential customers. Needless to say, every one of us was inspired and fired up from those speeches.

So, here's the thing, at the time, I felt intimidated. Just like Kurt said after my presentation, I figured I was too boring and would never be able to inspire people. I just didn't have the level of excitement that the speakers at the conference that day had. But this thought was far from the truth, and if your personality is more reserved and introverted, then I want you to hear this. Your style is yours alone, and there is always someone out there that will identify with it. So regardless of what type of crowd I'm speaking in front of or the size of the team I'm leading, I refuse to pretend to be some-one that I'm not. Some people may find my delivery and approach to be boring, and guess what...I may not be for them, and that's fine. Others will hear me and feel an instant connection, and that's fine too. Ultimately, we shouldn't care to be like or look like anyone else because it ends up being a waste of time. When we don't care about comparing ourselves to others, then we can step into our authentic selves. After all, the easiest person to be in this world is yourself.

LOVE YOURSELF

Ok, ok, I know... this is the section that sounds super cliché and reminds you of 1,000 other self-help books. The truth is that if we don't master this, then really, the rest of the words in this book don't matter. When you wake up in the morning, walk to the bathroom, and look in the mirror, what do you see? Happiness, failure, success, regret, joy, shame, hope, defeat? Have you thought about it lately, or maybe life is so busy that you're typically rushing and don't even have the 5 seconds that it takes to look at yourself? Or it could be that you avoid looking at yourself all together, afraid of what you might see and begin to think. Our lives become so busy with our daily routines that it's easy to lose sight of our own self-care. One book that was life-changing for me was 'Miracle Morning' by Hal Elrod. For me, one of the keys to starting off my day right is to have a solid morning routine where I can focus on self-empowerment. Now I know that everyone is not a morning person, so maybe your self-care time will be mid-morning, in the afternoon, or in the evening. I love the mornings because it gives me a catalyst to start my day off right. The perfect morning for me starts off like this: Miracle morning (1 hour)

Read bible scriptures and pray (15 minutes)

Exercise (30 minutes)

Meditate on goals for the day (15 minutes)

After that, it's time to take a shower, get my two toddlers up and ready, then the day gets started. Add to the routine above a fulfilling but healthy breakfast with fruit, protein, and fiber, and I'm good. Of course, sometimes life gets in the way, and I don't get to have the morning described above. What I know is that I've noticed a clear difference between how I feel when my day starts off this way versus when it doesn't. I feel energized, focused, reflective, and ready to take on the world. Conversely, when I haven't been eating right, haven't been getting proper sleep, haven't exercised, and haven't gone to church or read my bible in several weeks, I feel that too. Mentally I'm just not as sharp; it's like trying to put together a puzzle when several key pieces are missing. So, you can imagine how this carries over into my meetings with my team, my ability to make tough decisions, and my overall effectiveness as a leader. So having a self-care routine is all a part of loving yourself. This is so critical to being an effective leader because it plays into the confidence, or lack thereof, that you carry yourself with. Whatever the routine needs to be for you, it will be important to have and keep it consistent. I suggest setting alarms on your phone that remind you when it is time to start your routine each day, otherwise, life will get busy, and you'll always forget. I know because that is what used to happen to me.

As leaders, we have to fight off any negative thoughts or behaviors that could throw off our progress and impact our ability to lead. When you genuinely love who you are and take care of yourself, it also makes it much easier to be authentic because you don't care about the approval of anyone else. If you already have a balanced and consistent routine that gives you peace of mind to operate as your highest self, then congrats and keep it going! If not, then it's ok, think about something that you feel could work for you. The next time you look in the mirror, I want you to see a champion, a fighter, a winner. The truth is, if you don't believe it about yourself, then other people won't either. So, it all starts with you, be kind to yourself.

NEVER COMPROMISE YOUR INTEGRITY

I used to watch a show called American Greed on CNBC pretty regularly. The show highlights the stories of successful businessmen and business-women that had become multi-millionaires through building various business ventures. No matter how different each person's story was, there was always one common factor in everyone. The person being highlighted in the story had done something unethical in order to build their fortune. Whether it was scamming people into investing in ponzi schemes, representing professional athletes as a financial advisor, and then stealing millions from them, committing insurance fraud...the list goes on and on. At one point, these people were looked at with adoration and seemed to have a perfect life. Fast-forward to the police and federal prosecutors getting involved, sentences being handed down, and now that same person ends the episode in prison. It's a fascinating show because it shows just how quickly someone can rise to heights they would never have imagined and have it all come crashing down just as fast.

So, here's the question: what is your integrity worth? Let's bring it down several levels from the person that is swindling groups of people out of thousands and millions of dollars of their hard-earned money. Let's say you're in school and your friend tells you:

"Hey, I just got a copy of the test that's coming up next week. If you want, you can make a copy, you'll already have the answers and don't have to study".

Or you're at work, and your coworker says:

"You know they don't really check our timecards. If you leave an hour early and still log a full day of hours, it's cool. I do it all the time."

You might have a business arrangement where you and your partner share profit 50/50, one day a client writes you a check for a bonus on the side and says:

"You can keep this between us, this is just a little something extra for you. Your partner doesn't have to know about it."

So, what is your integrity worth? What are you willing to sell out for? A popular phrase says that integrity is what you do when nobody else is looking. Because let's be honest, in the majority of these scenarios, you could probably get away with doing the wrong thing at least once. In many cases in our lives, nobody may ever find out, period. But there is always a cost that comes with compromising your integrity. Let alone the consequences that come when you get caught, there's also the apathy that starts to grow in you over time. I don't think most of the people featured on American Greed started out with bad intentions in the very beginning, and I don't know any of them personally, so of course, I'm speculating. If I had to guess, I bet they were presented with a choice: take this one action, and although it is morally wrong, it will lead to you being successful beyond your wildest dreams. And that is the turning point, knowing what to do in that very moment. They probably had some apprehension at first, and questioned:

"Will I get caught? This doesn't seem right."

But they did it, got away with it, and on top of that, made money. Over time, with every deal and every transaction, they eventually are desensitized to it and don't even realize they're doing wrong anymore. It's the same way with us. Being an authentic leader that acts with integrity is not just about being morally sound with big decisions but knowing how to navigate all of the little ones. There will always be opportunities to cut corners to save money or to save time. If and when your team finds out that you are willing to do the wrong thing to get ahead, then the entire culture now changes. Remember, the team takes on the personality of the leader, so if they know that their leader is willing to take shortcuts, cheat the system and act without integrity, then guess what they'll do? In the event that your team never finds out about any of the wrongs you've done, then you still have to live with yourself and the guilt of knowing that you're a fraud. Either way, it's just not worth it. The wins in life are so much sweeter when they're done from a space of full transparency, honesty, and hard work.

So, to answer my own question earlier.... how much is my integrity worth? For me, there is no price, and I can't be bought. As leaders, we don't need anyone's approval, we don't need to take shortcuts to get ahead, and in the end, we can hold our heads high when we walk in our authentic truth.

WHAT INTROVERTS WISH EXTROVERTS KNEW

So here's the thing, if all that you think of me is that I'm quiet, reserved, or shy, then you don't know me. There are people that know another side of me, I just don't feel comfortable enough with you to show that. So you get a portion of me, but not the full thing. In order for me to feel comfortable to open up and be my authentic self around you, you can start by doing the following:

- When there's a conversation going on in a group setting, ask for my input. Don't just assume that because I'm being quiet it means I have nothing to say.
- When I speak, listen to what I say and acknowledge that you took in what I said.

These things probably seem small, but when you do it, I will notice and it increases the chances of you getting to know me.

PLAN OF ACTION

Never Compare Yourself to Anyone – Write a list of at least 3 things that you can be thankful for in your life right now. It doesn't have to be something major; it just has to mean something to you. Anytime you find yourself looking at or thinking about what someone else has, refer back to this list. You may want to keep a copy of the list with you at home or in your car on the way to work or to your business. As time goes on, continue to add to the list and revisit it frequently. Chances are, the more you look at and focus on what you already have, you'll spend way less time worrying about what you don't.

Love Yourself – What could a consistent self-care routine do for your life? If you've never had one or even thought about it, now is the time. Come up with a detailed plan that you can really start putting into action this week. You can determine when and how often to incorporate the routine into your schedule. It could be an hour in the morning, 30 minutes during lunchtime, 45 minutes in the evening before going to bed. Whatever works for you is fine; the key is to keep it consistent. Self-care can take on many forms because it's really about what brings you comfort. One approach is to divide it into categories; physical self-care (exercise, yoga), spiritual self-care (prayer, meditation), mental self-care (reading and writing). The key is to find the right approach that works for you.

Never Compromise Your Integrity – Think about a time in your professional or personal life where you had a decision that put your integrity on the line. Then think about any situations that you might currently be going through that could test your integrity. Now think about the possible consequences that could have resulted if you made the wrong decision in the past, and what could happen if you make the wrong decision now. If you've made decisions that compromised your integrity in the past, then hey, welcome to the club because I have too. Now is time to make the decision that from this day, you will walk in true integrity at all times.

CHAPTER 7
– COLLABORATION

"Be willing to be ok with not knowing things, be willing to not worry about the opinions of other people if you ask a question, and be willing to admit to others when they know more than you do."

I love to solve problems; it's probably why I fell in love with math and science at an early age. If you're reading this book and you have a pulse, then I'm sure you've probably figured out by now that life is full of problems, from the minor issues that we have to overcome day to day to the most critical and life-changing ones. We find ourselves in situations where we need to figure out what the next move will be that will get everything back on track. Depending on the severity of the problem, it can be extremely stressful and can start to dominate our thoughts. Whenever you're faced with a difficult problem in life, what is your first response? If your response is to tackle it by yourself, then you are wired like me. I went through the majority of my life trying to solve my own problems, regardless of what it was. If I'm being truthful, it wasn't just a love of solving problems that made me that way. It was also my pride. See, in my mind asking someone else for help equated to me admitting that I didn't know what I was doing. If I didn't know what I was doing, then people would sense that as a weakness, and the last thing I wanted was to be perceived as weak. Add to that my naturally introverted nature, where I enjoy the peace and solitude of working alone as opposed to a group. So, when tough times came up in life, I would just work through it. I had to keep up the image that I had it all together, and to people around me, they probably thought that I did.

If you ever thought that trying to solve all of life's problems by yourself somehow made you stronger, then I hate to break this to you, but it doesn't. In fact, you're literally making your life harder every single time that you attempt to solve a critical problem or make a critical decision without any counsel from other people. Sometimes introverts just don't want to be bothered with people or are so used to attacking the world alone that the concept of inviting someone else in to add input or critique our approach to things can be highly undesirable. If you're analytical like me, then you'd rather write down every step that needs to be taken to solve a problem on paper and begin to execute immediately. But I had to shift this way of thinking, and I have to continue to remind myself of it. As a leader when we run into difficult situations there is a key question that we should ask before attempting to do anything, that question is:

Who do I know that can help me with this?

If you're a student and you've been having trouble with math, instead of banging your head against the desk trying to figure out how to get each problem right, maybe you need a tutor. If you're a recent college graduate that started a job at a company and you're struggling to get up to speed on the new role, you might need a mentor that's been at the company for several years to show you the ropes. Or if you're thinking about getting married and have never done it before, it might be a good idea to talk to married couples and to look into marriage counseling. You get the point. It's a complete shift in mindset if you're used to living a life that's dependent on your efforts and your thoughts alone. Because leaders typically have significant responsibilities on a team, it becomes imperative that they're not the one that is doing everything. There must be a team in place, and the leader has to be willing to receive that help.

MY CAREER WAS JUST A PHONE CALL AWAY

In the fall of 2004, I left Tallahassee for the last time as a college student. I had failed an electromagnetic fields class with a D, which was literally the last credit that I needed to graduate with my Electrical Engineering degree. As a result, I'd walked across the stage in the fall 2004 Florida A&M graduation, but technically I still had one credit left to finish.

I packed up my Toyota Camry and started on the 13-hour drive back home to Dallas. I arrived without a job offer, without a degree, and with less than $100 to my name. I ended up moving back into my old room at my parent's house, focused on trying to get my life together. I remember talking to my dad and letting him know that I didn't intend to be there long. I realized it was time for me to grow up and make something happen. One of the first things I did was enroll in an Electromagnetic Fields class at the University of Texas Arlington for the spring semester; this was the one credit I needed to receive my degree. In addition to that, I was constantly looking at jobs and applying. I looked into every engineering field possible, some that didn't even have to do with my major. In the meantime, I didn't feel comfortable staying with my parents at the age of 23 with no job. So, while I waited on calls back from various companies, I decided to start applying for jobs at call centers. I ended up getting a job at a call center that did surveys for local businesses. It was a flexible job that I could work part-time.

Around the time I started working, was the same time that I started my Electromagnetic Fields class at UTA. So, my schedule for that spring consisted of applying for jobs during the day, driving 45 minutes each way from North Dallas to Arlington two nights a week for class, and working at the call center three nights a week and on the weekends. I'll never forget the first call that I got about an engineering opportunity. The company was PPG (Pittsburgh Plate and Glass). I got a call from their recruiter saying that they wanted to bring me in for an interview. The interview was at their plant in Wichita Falls, Texas. I got to meet several members of the team, including the person I would've been reporting to. I was at the site for about 3 hours, interviewing with different people. It felt like everything went really well. About 2 weeks later, I got a follow-up call from the same recruiter saying that they wanted to fly me up to their headquarters in Pittsburgh for a final round of interviews. I remember thinking, wow... this is really happening!

When I arrived in Pittsburgh, it was snowing heavily. The hotel they had reserved for me was downtown, and I'd never stayed in a hotel that was even close to being this nice. They'd paid for the round-trip plane ticket, the hotel and were even paying for my food. To me, I was living like a king. The PPG office was only a few blocks away from the hotel. I woke up early and started walking toward the office as snow continued to pour down. I got there and met the receptionist; she walked me to a waiting area where someone would come get me. There were three managers that got off of the elevator to approach me. We shook hands and walked to the interview room, where I handed each of them my resume as we sat down. After about 2 hours of discussion, the interview was over. We shook hands again, exchanged contact information, and even some parting laughs. The energy was great. As I walked back toward the hotel, I remember planning out what I would do with my first paycheck. First I'd get my apartment. Next I had to have a big-screen TV to watch my sports. Lastly I'd get a couch... to sit on while I watched my sports. I knew for sure I had the job. It was just a matter of it being official.

A week after returning from Pittsburgh, I hadn't gotten a call yet. They said I'd get a call within a week of the interview, but they were probably just busy and were working up the right offer for me, is what I told myself. Another day went by, then another...next thing I knew, another week had passed. I thought about reaching out to them but didn't want to bother them, so I decided to be patient. Then another week passed...every day without a phone call or email felt like a month. Finally, after over 3 weeks of waiting, I checked my email inbox one morning and saw an email from

PPG. This was it!! About time, let me see what salary offer I'll be getting, benefits, and everything else (of course, none of this mattered because I was going to accept anything they gave me). I opened the email and read the following:

Dear Mr. Terrance Lee,

We thank you for your interest in the Pittsburgh Plate Glass company. Unfortunately, we have decided to go in a different direction for this position. We appreciate your time and hope you will consider us for other opportunities in the future. In the meantime, feel free to apply for other positions on our website. Thank you.

I sat there for several minutes in my room, attempting to process what I'd just read. It didn't make sense to me; everything went perfectly in my visits to both sites. I'd done everything that I was taught to do in an interview. So, what happened? I had no idea, but what I did know was that this was a new low. I'd already told my parents about the job, and how sure I was that this was going to happen; I'd started looking into apartment complexes in Wichita Falls and in Pittsburgh, depending on which site I would end up at. My entire life had been planned out. I now had to tell my mom and dad that I didn't get the job, and the truth was that at the time, this was the only option I had on the table. I got dressed for work that night and drove to the call center where I was barely making over minimum wage, frustrated, angry, ashamed, and starting to have doubts about where my life was going.

A week after getting the news, I was sitting at my parent's house looking through jobs online. Then a thought suddenly came to me, a thought that truly felt supernatural and to this day I am convinced did not come from me. The thought simply said to make the call. What followed was an overwhelming feeling that whatever this call was, I had to make it right at that moment. I started thinking of what this could mean and who exactly I was supposed to call. Well, while I was at FAMU, I'd applied and was selected for the Emmett J Conrad Scholarship, which was a partial scholarship

offered by Senator Royce West's office in Dallas. This scholarship was crucial in helping to pay my tuition during my junior and senior years in
college. Anyway, I don't know why I didn't think to call them before. I
never thought about the fact that someone in that scholarship office might
have connections that could help get me a job. Regardless here I was sitting
in my room, and there was no denying what I'd heard, so I called the office.

A lady answered the phone, and I explained to her that I was a scholarship
recipient who had attended Florida A&M and was getting my final credit
for my degree at the University of Texas Arlington. I told her that I would
have my BS degree in Electrical Engineering in May; it was around early
March at the time. We talked for a few minutes, and she was very encouraging, almost in a motherly way. Looking back, she could probably hear
the desperation in my voice. She told me that she would ask around about
opportunities, I said thank you, and we hung up. I emailed her my resume
and went on about my day thinking that I probably wouldn't hear from
them again.

About a week later, I saw that I had a missed call and voicemail from a
number I didn't recognize. The voicemail was from a lady named Tenequa Moffit, a recruiter with Lockheed Martin. She said that she'd received
a copy of my resume, and they wanted to bring me in for an interview.
I called her back immediately. She explained that they had received my
resume from the lady at the scholarship office a few days ago and asked if
I could come onsite for an in-person interview next week. We scheduled
a time for the interview and hung up. Next week came; I got dressed in
the one suit that I had and headed to Fort Worth, where the Lockheed
Martin plant was located. There I met the manager of the team I would
be interviewing with, Roland Williams. It was another student that had
graduated from Purdue University named Nick Kuhntz and me. We spent
about a half-day touring the facility, interviewing and meeting members
of the team. When it was over, I shook Roland's hand and thanked him for
the opportunity. However, the feeling was completely different than when

I'd left the interview with PPG. I assumed that I wasn't going to get the job. Part of it was the letdown I'd already experienced and not wanting to get my hopes up too high. I went to work that night like it was a regular day, expecting to get a similar rejection email to the one I'd gotten before.

A few weeks after the interview, I was on campus at UTA studying for an upcoming exam. It was now early April 2005. While sitting outside the library, I got a phone call, I answered, and the person was from Lockheed Martin. The next sentence is one that I'll never forget:

"Mr. Lee, the team really liked you. We'd like to offer you a position as a system engineer with our F-16 team in Fort Worth, TX. An offer letter with the starting salary has been sent to your email. You'll have a week to accept or decline the offer. Congratulations, do you have any questions?"

I don't even remember what I said. What I wanted to say was:

"Yes, I accept! I'll start tomorrow!"

I hadn't even read my email to see the salary yet, and truthfully, I didn't care. We got off the phone, and I sat there for a few minutes, overcome with emotion. The next thing that I had to do was to call the people that had helped get me to this point. I called Senator Royce West's scholarship office. I didn't know the name of the lady that I spoke to before, and a different person answered the phone this time when I called. I told them that I'd just got a job with Lockheed Martin, and I wanted to thank them for helping me out. My next call was to Tenequa Moffit, the recruiter at Lockheed Martin, who had taken my resume and set up my interview. I called the number for the recruiting office, and someone else answered. They informed me that I wasn't able to speak with Tenequa because she had just left the company last week.

So, here's the thing.... I had an urge that day to make a call, so I did. Had I waited a few more weeks or a month to make that same call, then Tenequa would have no longer been there, and I most likely would have never got an interview with Lockheed Martin. If I'd never gotten an interview with Lockheed Martin, then I most likely wouldn't have ended up starting my career as an engineer in the defense industry in 2005. If I'd never started off my career in defense, then I wouldn't be here writing this book 15 years later that is based off of real-life lessons that I've learned on leadership. Now for some of you reading that, you're probably thinking, "Man, you were lucky that you called when you did!" But for me, there were just too many coincidences and no possible way that I could've planned out what happened. To this day, I believe it was God pushing me towards my purpose, and part of the lesson was that it's ok to rely on people. It taught me that I no longer had to go through life alone.

THREE PILLARS OF COLLABORATION

THE POWER OF "I DON'T KNOW"

You ever ask somebody a question, and as soon as they start talking, you can tell they don't really know the answer? Have you ever had that know it all co-worker, family member, or friend that acts like they know everything? It doesn't matter what you or anyone else in the room asks; that person always appears to have an answer lined up. They've somehow managed to travel to every country in the world, eaten at every restaurant you ever mention and are the first to jump in with an answer for any question that's ever asked in a conversation. Something that people like that rarely think about and probably aren't aware of is this, most of the time, we can tell if that person is lying or putting on a front. It's a common thing to do, and honestly, it's the way that many humans interact. We want to appear to be smart, well cultured, and to always have something to contribute to the conversation. You don't see people post or comment on social media admitting what they don't know about a topic. That would go against one of the fundamental purposes of social media, which is to provide other people with our daily highlight reel.

Admitting that you don't know something can be hard, but the irony is that there is extreme power in it. Think about a scenario where you're at a dinner party with a group of friends. Someone brings up a trip that they'll be taking to Spain in the upcoming months. They are excited talking about all of the details surrounding the trip. Other people at the table start talking about the various things they've heard about the country, and one couple that has been there starts to talk about their personal experiences. Your friend that's going turns to you and asks,

"Hey, what have you heard about Spain? Do you know anyone that's been?"

You say, *"Oh yeah, I know plenty of people who have been there. I was actually thinking about going next year."*

The truth is, you haven't had a single thought about anything having to do with Spain, but you were feeling left out of the conversation, so you said something. The conversation moves on to other topics. What if when your friend asked the question, your response was something like this,

"You know, I've never been to Spain, but I'd love to learn more about the people and the culture. Can you send me some info on the country? Let me know how your experience was when you get back!"

Your friend now starts to look in their phone for links to various websites and blog posts with information about the country. They start sending everything to you from places to eat, historical landmarks to visit, and best times of the year to go. You then start doing your own research, and the next thing you know, you've learned more about Spain in a few days than you knew your entire life. You end up deciding that you want to take a trip to the country, so you start saving and planning the time of the year that you plan to go. A few months pass, and one day you're on the way to the airport about to board a flight to Spain. This single thought was planted in your head from one conversation. If you had acted like you knew what your friend was talking about, then they never would have bothered to send you the information that they did. If they had never done that, then you wouldn't have started to read and research the country, which eventually inspired you to go.

This is obviously a random example, but this plays out in our lives all of the time. How many times in school has a teacher asked, "So does anyone have any questions on the material I just went over?" and you didn't raise your hand. How many times have you been in a meeting at work and the person leading it asks, "Ok, so now that we've discussed the new approach for this project, is everyone aware of what we're looking to accomplish here?" and you sat there silent looking around to see if anyone else would speak up. Listen, questions are a sign of intelligence. When we discover that there is something we don't know, we should become obsessed with learning it. And when we find out who the person is that is the guru on a topic, we should have no shame in falling back and becoming a student. Now granted, to be a leader in your field, you do have to become knowledgeable about your craft. If your teammates are asking you 20 questions per day and you only know the answer to 1 of them, then you might be in the wrong role. But the reality is, no matter how knowledgeable you think that you are, you'll never know everything. Be willing to be ok with not knowing things, be willing to not worry about the opinions of other people if you ask a question, and be willing to admit to others when they know more than you do.

WHO'S ON YOUR TEAM?

One skill that exceptional leaders have is the ability to identify things they are good at and to rely on other people for everything else. It's also been said that if you're sitting in a room and you are the smartest person there, then you're in the wrong room. There can be an ego boost that comes with feeling like we're always the smart one in our circle, even if we're not the most talkative. The problem with this is that we're not being challenged, and as a result, we remain in our bubble where we are only exposed to what we know. It can be easy to continue going through life this way, especially for many introverts. But if we are going to be leaders, then we must learn how to focus on building great teams.

Now I know that for some of you reading this, that might sound like something that is meant for an extrovert to do. But team building is something that can not only be done by an introverted leader, but can be done well. This is where you can use your natural skills to observe, listen and read people. You will have an advantage here because while other people might be quick to make team-building decisions, you will be thinking deeply about who the best people are for the team and how well they would work together. The first step, though, is to admit that you need a strong team in the first place because as we mentioned in the previous pillar, you're not going to know everything. A strong team will free you from so much pressure, allowing you time to focus more on other things.

When I was in my first rotation of the Engineering Leadership Development Program at Lockheed Martin, I pretty much stayed at my desk and worked unless it was time for a meeting. I was helping with a research and development project and was working under a good project lead named Jeff that had given me a clear objective for what I needed to accomplish during my rotation. It was a complex project in many ways; oftentimes if I had questions, I would go to him. But there was a team of engineers in the area that were working on the same project that I rarely interacted with. Several of them had extensive experience in the industry and probably could've answered almost any question that I had. When I would hit a roadblock or had a question, instead of building relationships with the other engineers, I would typically try to figure it out myself if Jeff wasn't available. Also, when it was time to go to lunch, one of the engineers would ask if I wanted to go to the cafeteria, and I would always decline. Usually, I would go eat with a friend of mine that worked outside of the group or just eat lunch at my desk. I didn't realize it at the time, but I had essentially put myself on an island. I was sitting in a room of over 10 engineers every day for months but was never really a part of the team. Essentially, we were a team by location because we sat together, but there was no real interaction between them and me.

At the end of my rotation, my manager Susan gave me that feedback, that she didn't feel like I had become a part of the team and that if I wanted to be a leader, I couldn't just sit at my desk. She explained to me that leadership was an interactive sport, and I had been on the sidelines. In fact, of the over 20 ELDP students that were in our rotational program, it was clear that I was the one that was not into networking with other people. I thought to myself, well, sorry, but that's just not me. If I have to attend lunches that I don't want to go to and always be talking to people, then I may not be able to lead people. That was in 2013. I remember what she told me, and I'm thankful that she did. My mentality has changed completely since that time. When I realize I have a gap in knowledge with something, my very first question is,

"Who do I know that can help with this?"

It doesn't matter how smart you are; you are not going to know everything. You also don't want to put the pressure on yourself of feeling like you have to know everything and be able to solve every problem. The teams that I currently work with as a project manager and engineering manager are extremely diverse. No one person knows everything about the products that we support, but everyone on the team has something significant that they can contribute to the larger goal. But this starts with building a team of strong people and being willing to accept help from that team. It is also true that relationships are built through conversation and time spent together. Going to lunch together and going to social outings away from work help with getting to know the people that you work with. Asking people how they're doing and genuinely listening to them talk about what happened over their weekend, their families, and their challenges do more to build a relationship than sitting in a meeting room. If you're an introvert, then you may not always be in the mood to do this, so the key is to find your balance between constant social interaction and becoming the person that only speaks to people in a meeting. It is critical that your team knows you and trusts you. So while you don't have to completely become an extrovert in a social sense, you will need to build a relationship with your teammates. Whatever it is that you're trying to accomplish, having the right team in place that is built around a culture of trust and respect will make a world of difference.

THE ART OF DELEGATION

Having a team is great, but it doesn't benefit you in the long run if you're still the person that does everything. Let me be the first to raise my hand and say that I'm talking to myself with this one. Even when I have a team in place, I oftentimes will still try to do way too much. However, having a strong work ethic doesn't have to translate into you doing all of the work. Teams are put in place for us to be able to leverage each other. Here's a scenario:

You log in to your email on a Monday morning. After going through your emails and looking at your open action list from last week, you have 10 things that absolutely have to be done by the end of the day. On top of that, you have several meetings lined up throughout the day, so how is it even possible for you to get all of this done? As someone that is routinely in the scenario mentioned above, the answer is going to be one of three options:

1) You work yourself tirelessly in between meetings or during meetings, if necessary, to get the 10 items done. More than likely, a few of the items won't get your full attention since you'll be rushing through them, which means there will likely be re-work on some of the actions.
2) You look at the list of 10 items and identify which of them can be done by somebody else and which ones you should do.
3) The list doesn't get done.

I'm happy to say that as of the writing of this book, I am slowly transitioning into number 2 above, although it is a struggle! When you work on certain things that you enjoy, that thing can begin to feel like your baby. A concept for a business is often like this or a project at work or school that you've invested countless hours into. You trust yourself, but you don't know if you can trust somebody else to treat that project or 'baby' the same way that you would. And this is understandable; after all, you have put a lot of work and effort into seeing it through. What you don't want to happen is the thing that inevitably happens whenever someone takes on all of the challenges, issues, headaches, and hard work needed to make something successful by himself or herself. And that is burnout, I know, because I've been there. Most of us have busy lives, and leaders know that it's impossible to get everything done without help.

So when you make your to-do list for the day or for the week, instead of stressing about how many things you have to get done, look at every item and determine if you have to be the person to do it. This leadership pillar of delegation ties in closely with the first two of admitting what you don't know and building a strong team. When you analyze your list of actions, look to distinguish the ones that are the easiest for you from the ones that are outside of your area of expertise. If there is any task where you know someone that could finish it in 30 minutes, as opposed to you spending 2 hours on it, then delegate it to that person. This will not only save you time and energy, but it is also empowering for the person that you're delegating to. When you delegate to someone, you are displaying the fact that you trust them, and this goes a long way with people. Of course, successful delegation can't be accomplished if you don't have the right team in place, so this is where careful team building becomes so important.

As a functional manager, one of the things that is always in the back of my mind when I'm interviewing someone is this; what unique skill or ability would this person bring to our team that we don't already have? Think about your current pain points; what are the things on your to-do list that you absolutely dread doing. Every time you think about starting it, you find yourself procrastinating and pushing it off until tomorrow, or next week, or next month. Why not find someone that thrives in doing tasks like that? You get to delegate to them, which frees you of pressure, and they get to perform a task that they love. This creates a win-win scenario for everyone. When you start to embrace the art of delegation, you will find yourself slowly feeling freer, more relaxed, and in control. As a leader, you don't have to feel like the weight of the world is on your shoulders when you have a team of great people there to share the weight with you.

WHAT INTROVERTS WISH EXTROVERTS KNEW

I oftentimes prefer to work alone, and feel my most productive in this setting. But I also realize that I can't do everything by myself, so if I need to work with a team then I will need to feel free to be myself. So while you might feel that our team is most productive working together in the same room, while brainstorming ideas on a white board, I may only be able to do that for a period of time. I might require the freedom to break away from the group from time to time to collect my thoughts, to work in solitude, and then come back to the group setting. Trust me, I will be most productive when you allow me to work in an environment that fits my personality. So it's not that I won't collaborate and won't be a team player, because I will. I just need the flexibility to do it on my terms.

PLAN OF ACTION

The Power of "I don't know" – The next time you're in a room with your friends, family, co-workers, or business partners, make a conscious effort to listen closely during the conversation. If you hear someone bring up a topic or ask a question that you don't know anything about, ask that person to explain more about it. As they are talking, be sure to listen with intention and take notes on what is being said. The point is to get into the mindset of admitting when others know more than you and opening up your mind to exploring new things.

Who's on your team? – Write down the names of the 5 people that you spend the most time working with every day. Next, write down one strength that each of those people has that you don't. Spend some time reviewing your list and begin to think about ways that you can leverage their talents to make your team more successful in the future. Keep this list for reference so that when your team runs into challenging situations, you'll know which people on your team are best to have assigned to various tasks.

The Art of Delegation – What are 5 things in your life that are on your to-do list to get done and are causing you the most concern right now? It could be trying to sort through over 100 emails at work and address the actions in those emails, a business that you would like to launch but get intimidated when you see all of the tasks you'll need to finish to get started, or maybe something as simple as trying to get all of your errands done for your house in a short time span. Whatever it is, write down these 5 things, and next to each one, write down the name of someone else that might be able to help you with it. As a leader, it is critical that you get out of the mindset of needing to be the one to execute everything. That's what your team is for.

CHAPTER 8 – CONFIDENCE

"Regardless of what you may believe about yourself, you have the power to be a force in front of a room."

It's consistently been rated as one of the top fears among people regardless of social class, race, religion, or age. For some people, it's an afterthought that is done effortlessly with little thought or concern. For others, the mere anticipation of it causes nerves to spike, hands to sweat, and minds to fill with terror. That thing is public speaking. Whether it's a kid giving their easter speech in front of a church, a college student presenting their team project in an auditorium, the big presentation that someone has to give at a meeting for work, or the pitch that the business owner needs to give potential investors the skill of public speaking is imperative for those who desire to lead. When conversations about public speaking come up, most people picture a large packed room with hundreds of people and one person standing at a microphone in preparation to speak. But in reality, for some people, a room with no more than 3 to 5 people in it can be intimidating to stand up and talk in front of, even if the people in that room are friends or family. If this sounds like you in anyway, then first of all, I want you to know that you are not alone. This is probably one of the chapters in this book that I am the most passionate about because I can identify so closely with it.

So, the million-dollar question, if you have this fear, how do you get over it? Well, here's my thought, and I'm sure there will be people who disagree with me, and that's fine. The truth is you may never completely get over it. I am a functional manager of an engineering team with over 20 people, a project manager with the responsibility of tracking tasks for over 30 engineers, and routinely have to brief executive level leaders, and I still get nervous before some presentations. If you thought you were picking up this book to hear from someone that has mastered the craft of speaking and is always 100% confident before addressing a room full of people, then hey, I'm sorry to disappoint you. I routinely find myself using the pillars outlined in this chapter to keep myself grounded and focused anytime I have to address a group of people. Even with that, ironically, these days, I enjoy expressing my opinion in challenging situations and can't wait to share my thoughts with my teammates. Recently I've also discovered that whenever there's a chance to speak in front of a crowd, no matter how small or how large, I typically seize it. I honestly don't even know why.... but I actually enjoy it now, maybe because I spent so much of my life in fear of it. Who would've thought the laid-back introverted guy would be the one who gets joy out of speaking and helping people with their public speaking skills?

With that said, don't take this to mean that I snapped my fingers one day and was able to address crowds with thousands of people with the smoothness and charisma of a Barack Obama. That's not what I'm saying (but hey, maybe one day). What I'm saying is that by learning and applying the skills that we're going to discuss in this chapter, I was able to not beat the fear of public speaking but to embrace it. The fear of what others might be thinking when I'm talking, the fear that I might mess up, the fear that I'm not good enough to even be talking in front of this room of people. Again, I still get nervous from time to time, that may never go away. But I don't run from the fear anymore, I face it head-on, and I love it. I look forward to working together to get over this fear if you do have it. Regardless of what you may believe about yourself, you have the power to be a force in front of a room.

SINK OR SWIM

Sometimes you're put in situations in life where you only have two simple choices; to sink or to swim. Early on in my engineering career, I quickly found myself in that position.

I was about 1 year into my first engineering job, and at the time, was shadowing a senior engineer named Brian Fields. Now, this guy was smart, and when I say smart, I mean next-level smart. There was a particular capability on the aircraft we were developing that he was the subject matter expert for, and I was working to gain as much knowledge from him as possible. We would spend time during work hours and after normal work hours, writing on his whiteboard about various mission scenarios and design concepts for us to consider. I would sit there with my notebook taking as many notes as possible and asking tons of questions. I was essentially a sponge just taking in everything. One day Brian came in and told the team that he would be leaving our division for an opportunity in California. He would be transitioning off the team in about 3 weeks. I was happy for him and his new opportunity until I remembered something. There was a systems requirement review meeting scheduled for about a month from then. This was a meeting where the lead system engineer would brief the systems engineering team, software engineers, integration and test engineers, and pilots on the new design concept and any changes to existing system architecture. I thought to myself,

"Sooooo, who's going to do the brief?"

At the time, I was the only engineer on the team that had been spending a significant amount of time with Brian and the only one who had been tracking the design updates that he had been working on. I don't remember who told me, whether it was Brian or my manager at the time, but I was informed that I would have to lead the brief.

I was terrified.... the presentation was several weeks away, and I was already talking myself out of it. I pictured a room of 30 or more people staring at me while I, a kid fresh out of college, fumbled over my words and struggled. Everyone would leave the meeting feeling like I didn't know what I was talking about, and people would be making jokes about it over lunch. That's what was going on in my head. I had created the entire scenario. As time got closer to the presentation, Brian continued to help me put the slides together and shared as much knowledge with me as he could before it was time for him to go. He taught me more in those few weeks about the system I would be briefing than I would've thought possible. I'm incredibly thankful to him for that. In addition, another coworker, Robbie Vaughn, was extremely knowledgeable on the system I would be briefing as well. She also spent time with me before the day of the presentation. We went over the material that I would be presenting together several times. She would offer suggestions to me for how to deliver my message and how to make my presentation easier to understand. The morning of the review came; by this time, Brian had left our group and was now in California, so I no longer was able to walk over to his cube and ask questions, something I would frequently do before. However, Robbie was still there, and I knew she would be at the presentation, so that was a good feeling.

I got to the room early to set up, and Robbie sat next to me as people started to walk in and fill the room. When the room was full of over 30 engineers and pilots, it was now time to start. Feeling extremely tense, I took a deep breath, welcomed everybody to the meeting, and started my presentation. Then the strangest thing happened. I felt very shaky at first, my voice cracked a few times, but after the first minute or two of talking, I was fine. My nerves calmed, and my voice started to strengthen. I sat up straight in my chair and was delivering my message to the team. There were several tough questions throughout the meeting that the team had for me; after all, it was a complex project I was briefing them on. I was able to answer some of the questions, but for the ones that I didn't know, Robbie was right there to back me up. Before I knew it, the presentation was over, a few people told me 'great job', including Robbie. I'll never forget her telling me how calm I was while presenting and that most new hires would have been too nervous about presenting in a room full of people like that. I told her "thank you" while thinking to myself..." I've been worried sick about this day for the past 3 weeks!"

It ended up being a great day, and her saying that did something for me. I hadn't turned into some master communicator overnight, but I had gained some level of confidence. A confidence that I could speak in a room full of extremely smart people and hold my own. I didn't know it at the time, but this was a huge milestone for me. However, I'd been put in a situation where I had to perform under pressure before, and the experience was equally as nerve wracking.

WHEN PRACTICE PAYS OFF

When I was a junior in high school, I was part of an organization called Jack and Jill of America, my parents were members in the North Dallas chapter. We used to have yearly conferences in the summer, and one of the events during the conference was a speech competition. Somehow, I got signed up, then found out that I would be giving a speech at the regional conference and had to come up with a topic. It was the summer after my junior year going into my senior year, and all I and my friends would talk about was how college was going to be. I chose for the topic of my speech "Preparing for College."

My mom reached out to a good family friend of ours, Mrs. Carolyn Mccloud, to help me prepare for my presentation. Mrs. Mccloud was an educator like my mom and had a big personality like my mom too. I started writing my speech and going over to Mrs. Mccloud's house to practice for it. She would give me feedback on several things, such as not staring down at the paper but scanning the crowd and making eye contact, what to do with my hands while I was talking, my voice inflection, and making sure that I project my voice. In addition, she made several edits to my speech along the way. Educators truly have a way of catching and seeing things that you just don't see. I would think I had written something incredible, and she would strike through it and re-word it. However, anytime she would do this, the sentence would sound better than what I'd had before. She was very good. She practiced and worked with me over a period of about a month until eventually, it was time for the conference. The speech competition was in the ballroom of a hotel. There were students from all over Texas and Louisiana there, well over 300 people. The students that were competing all sat at the front of the stage at a long table. I sat there next to 5 other students; I would be representing our North Dallas chapter. As other students were going through their presentations, I was looking out to the crowd and trying to mentally prepare myself for when my name would get called to go up to the stage.

I would occasionally sip some of the water that was in front of me at the table. In a moment of clumsiness, I made a quick motion with my hand and accidentally hit the glass of water in front of me. Some of the water spilled out right onto the printed-out speech that I was about to give. I was able to catch the glass from spilling out completely onto my entire speech, but the water that did get on the pages was starting to smear the ink, and it was making parts of my speech impossible to read. There were even a few girls sitting in the front row that saw me spill the water, one of whom I had a little crush on. Of course, I tried to play it off and act cool, like it didn't happen...but when I looked up, I saw her and her friends looking right at me. Talk about embarrassing. Anyway, it got to less than a minute to go before my speech, I looked down at my papers, and by this point, the smearing of the ink had spread. Out of my 3-page speech, about half of it was unreadable. Before I knew it,

"Next up, from the North Dallas Chapter of Jack and Jill America, we'll hear a speech from Terrance Lee" **crowd applauds**.

I nervously started walking up to the stage with my water-soaked speech. Then, one of the weirdest things happened that, to this day, I can't really explain. The first part of my speech was readable, so I was able to look down at my notes to get started. But about 30 seconds into my speech, I realized that I didn't really need my notes anymore. I gave the rest of the speech without reading from the paper. There's actually a video of it that my parents have to this day. In the video, you see me looking down at times at my paper, but the paper was basically smeared ink! See, Mrs. Mccloud had taught me not to trust my notes and to be overly prepared. We had gone over the speech so many times that by this point, it was ingrained in my head. She taught me the importance of proper preparation and the amount of practice that you must commit to if you are going to excel. I am incredibly grateful today for that lesson.

THREE PILLARS OF CONFIDENCE

WHEN YOU GET NERVOUS

Getting nervous when you're about to speak in front of people is common, don't let anyone ever make you feel like something is wrong with you for feeling that way. But once you acknowledge it for what it is, then it's time to defeat it. Our nervousness comes from fear, which we project internally on ourselves or we have projected externally from others. That fear can cause mental roadblocks that will attack our confidence or even physical reactions like sweating, shakiness in our voice, and others. Mine is that I feel my heart start to beat fast, which is very weird, but it just happens, and I can't explain it. Even as I sit here writing this book, I recently led a briefing and felt that feeling right before it was my turn to present. You might have thought that you would read this chapter and hear me promise that after reading this, you'll never be nervous talking in front of people again. The reality is I can't promise you that, and it would be wrong of me to do so. What I can promise is that if you identify what your triggers are and utilize the tips given in this chapter to deal with them, then you will absolutely improve your chances for success and will no longer be dominated by your fear.

Control Your Breathing

If your heart starts racing, you feel your throat start to clam up, or you get a nervous feeling in your stomach when you're about to speak in front of a crowd, try taking deep breathes. Although I find myself presenting information to teams almost daily, from time to time, I still get the accelerated heartbeat that I described above. When this happens, I pause and breathe deeply for about 10 to 15 seconds. Other people in the room can never tell when I'm doing this, and they would never know. These 10 to 15 seconds can do wonders for calming your nerves. If you are feeling overly anxious prior to speaking, then you'll slowly start to feel yourself calming down. It also can help to clear your mind of any negative thoughts and allow you to focus on what you're about to say.

Laugh

When you're standing in front of a room full of people, or are preparing to speak on a conference call with several people on, you want to win over the room, and you want to put yourself at ease as well. One way to immediately calm your nerves and to release tension is to get a good laugh. If you're nervous when you first start speaking, then this is a good way to break the ice and help to calm you down. Of course, it depends on the audience and subject matter that you're speaking about. If you're about to deliver the news in a meeting to one of your suppliers that your company is firing them, then that might not be the time for a knock-knock joke. You have to know your audience to be able to gauge if this will be considered appropriate or not. You don't have to be a standup comedian or anything. It might be as simple as starting off your speech or presentation with a witty, sarcastic remark. Something that will get a few chuckles from the people you're talking to. The key is to be yourself, don't try to force a laugh, and don't try to act like anyone else while doing this. This is about you being your authentic self and hopefully getting a few smiles from your audience in the process. The other option that you can do regardless of the situation is to think of a funny joke or funny moment in your head. Sometimes just having a humorous thought is enough to put you at ease. So remember, smile, laugh, have fun, and don't take yourself too seriously! It will definitely help.

Master Your Body Language

There have been several studies conducted on communication, and how much of it is verbal (what is actually being said) versus non-verbal (vocal tones and visual cues). The overwhelming majority of these studies have concluded that an audience that listens to someone speak will take away significantly less of what the person actually said than that person's vocal inflection and body language. Some studies have even suggested that verbal communication is less than 10% of a conversation. So there is no denying the importance of body language in communication. You're going to project the energy that you give out, and this is where non-verbal communication is key. If you're sitting at the table with your coworkers, business partners, fellow students, or anyone else, and you are sitting with your shoulders slumped down, head tilted downwards, and avoiding looking people in the eye, then you are giving off the perception of not being confident. If you're at that same table sitting up straight in a posture that says you're ready to engage in discussion, if your head is held up high, and you're making eye contact with each person at the table, then you will give off the perception of confidence to the other people in the room and most importantly to yourself. Your posture is equally important if you're standing in front of a room of people to speak. Be sure to stand tall, survey the crowd, keep your hands actively moving and not in your pockets, and project your voice properly for the crowd. As you do these things, you will feel the difference, and your nervousness will start to melt away because your posture and your mindset will now be aligned for you to win.

Find a friendly face in the crowd

It might be a friend, it might be the person you were having small talk with before it was your turn to speak, or maybe it's the one person that you notice is consistently nodding their head in agreement as you're talking. In order to engage and win over your audience, it's important that you're scanning the room as you're talking and making eye contact with as many people in the room as you can while doing it. However, I've always found it helpful to lock in on one to two people in the audience that you've won over. If you start to feel anxious about all of the eyes that are on you at any point, you know that you can always turn your attention and eye contact back to that person for some relief. At the same time, be careful not to focus completely on them, as you can then risk losing the rest of the room. This is all about making yourself comfortable, so if you feel your nerves starting to spike, you can always go back to that friendly face, and engage with them.

Hopefully, you will find those tips to be helpful. Again, I want to repeat this, if you get nervous or start to feel anxious whenever you have to speak in front of people, I am with you. You are not weird, and you are not alone. You have something important to say, and the world can't wait to hear it, so I'm rooting for you.

Practice, Practice, Practice

Let's face it, the best way to get better at anything is to do it over and over again. There's just no other way. Depending on your situation, there are probably groups you can join that will help with this. One organization that I strongly recommend is Toastmasters. For a short period of time when I was in my first engineering role out of school, I attended Toastmasters meetings for a few months. The thing that I found beneficial about it was the fact that I was around people like me. Everyone there was trying to become a better speaker and had insecurities they were dealing with. So, there were no judgments or expectations; everyone there made you feel welcome. Most important, it gave me hours and hours of practice speaking in front of people, which is really what I needed. All of the advice about how to do something sounds great in a book like this, but until you go out and apply it, nothing changes.

You need to make it a goal to put yourself in a position to speak in front of people as much as possible. If there is no Toastmasters organization in your area, then maybe you can start with a local group of friends or family members. Ask them if you can start practicing speaking in front of them. This can easily be done in your living room, their living room, wherever it really doesn't matter. The point is that it's going to build up hours of practice. When I was in network marketing, my business partners and I would literally practice the same presentation over and over for hours. During this time, we would give each other critique and constructive criticism.

By the time we had a business meeting, and one of us had to present to prospective clients, we all knew the presentation material like the back of our hand.

This is also a reason that practice and preparation are so important. Have you ever sat through a meeting or been in a class for school, and somebody reads word for word off of a PowerPoint slide? If people are just going to have the slide read to them, they can do that themselves. This is a clear giveaway that someone is not comfortable with the material that they're briefing. A PowerPoint slide is just a means to get a message across. It is not the lifeblood of a presentation. When people are at a function or in a meeting, they are there to hear what you as the speaker have to say. And if you've gone over your material countless times, then it will be second nature to you when you're briefing it in front of other people.

Another thing that is critical when presenting information is to anticipate the hard questions. For example, you're giving a presentation at work, and on the first slide, you have a bullet that states:

"Company sales have decreased by 30% this quarter."

If you pull up your slide deck and start briefing it, if I'm sitting in the room when I see that bullet, I immediately start thinking;

"Why did sales decrease?"

Then I think:

"What are you and your team doing to correct that going forward?"

Along with a number of other questions. As you're practicing your presentation or your pitch, be looking for areas where someone could potentially ask you a question. If you were looking at the presentation yourself, what questions would you ask? Make sure you know what these potential questions are ahead of time. That way, you're already prepared with the answers. Again this is a skill that comes with repetition and practice. You will get to a point where you will already know the questions that are coming ahead of time. And in the event that you're asked a question while you're presenting that you don't know the answer to, there's an approach for that too. What you absolutely do not want to do is pretend that you know; that's a recipe for disaster. You simply promise to follow-up with that person. This can sound like,

"Well, honestly, I don't have that answer at the moment. However I'm going to reach out to my (co-worker, business partner, or insert name) and will have an answer for you by the end of the day."

When someone asks you a question, all they really want is to be assured that they will get the question answered at some point, it doesn't always have to be in that moment. The next key is to be sure to keep your promise and follow-up with that person as soon as you have the answer they were looking for. Ultimately the more practice that you get speaking, the better off you'll be when handling scenarios like these. And you'll discover that the nervousness that once controlled your entire being will no longer hold you hostage. So, put in the time and put in the effort. You'll be amazed at the results.

WHAT'S YOUR MANTRA?

Sometimes the most important words that we ever say are the ones we tell ourselves. A therapist recently explained the difference to me between the brain and the mind. The brain is a physical organ that is located in your head, which is made up mostly of soft tissue, nerve cells, and blood vessels. It is an organ that you need to live, just like your heart, liver, intestines, and other functioning organs. However, the mind is something completely different. The mind is the playground for your thoughts, your imagination, your dreams, and your nightmares. Within the mind lies our morality for whether we'll make good or bad decisions, our judgments, and bias toward other people, our romantic thoughts about our significant others. One person's mind and another person's, will be completely different, and there is no way to see it.

The interesting concept that the therapist proposed to me was about how to use my mind to retrain my brain. The way he described it when we have self-limiting thoughts, those thoughts are wiring our brain to react a certain way. However, the good news is that we can flip this. So, what would happen if instead of focusing on everything that could go wrong when I go in front of people to speak, I focus on everything that could go right? I envision everyone that I'm talking to nodding their heads in agreement and responding to my presentation with warm-hearted smiles and applause. With this thinking, my mind over time is now forcing my brain to be rewired. Now I will not only feel confident, but it will literally become the default attitude that I have in any situation because my mind is now consumed with positive thinking.

There are things that we're told as kids that can still affect us as adults for good and for bad. I've had friends who have experienced physical and verbal abuse; it's heartbreaking to hear some of the stories about how it affected their confidence. What we often fail to realize is that our self-talk can sometimes be equally just as abusive. When you have to give a presentation, stand up in front of a classroom, give a speech at a family function, or any other scenario where you are front and center with a crowd, what's going through your mind? Are you thinking,

"I hope I don't screw this up"

"I'm not ready for this"

or anything similar? Do you start to feel nervous and feel like everyone else in the room will be able to tell how nervous you are, as if they can look into your thoughts and read your mind? Whatever you've been telling yourself when it is your time to speak in front of people, if it is negative, then today is the day that it ends. You will no longer be a captive to fear. The key is to replace your destructive self-talk with positive thoughts. This is why I like the concept of having a mantra; it's a place that you can go to mentally whenever you need an escape. For me, I came up with two that I regularly use if I ever get into a situation where I start to feel nervous or worried about public speaking. The first one is my favorite bible verse, Philippians 4:13, which reads, "I can do all things through Christ who strengthens me." I'll repeat this verse in my head, and immediately, I feel powerful. If my nerves were bad, then they slowly start to calm down. My other one is a simple phrase where I repeat, "I am the best speaker in the room." With every repetition of this phrase, I begin to feel the calmness take over my being, and the nervousness fades.

I don't know what the right self-talk will be for you, but you need to have something. Now I'll admit that at one point, I had to do this exercise before any type of presentation regardless of how big or small the audience is. These days I don't have to do it nearly as much, but I always listen and pay close attention to my self-talk. If I ever feel myself getting nervous, I immediately start repeating my mantras; it's become second nature for me now. Whatever you decide your mantra will be, get in the practice of repeating it before any big presentation (to yourself, of course). I realize this may sound silly, and it seems like there are a million self-help gurus that have said this and have talked about how your thoughts become manifested in real life. But I can honestly say that this makes a difference. Be kind to yourself, believe in yourself, and speak life to yourself.

WHAT INTROVERTS WISH EXTROVERTS KNEW

If I shy away from, get nervous or have reservations about speaking in front of a group it does not make me weak or helpless. And if you find public speaking to be easy and not a big deal, then guess what, for me it is and there's nothing wrong with that. With the proper tools, coaching and practice I can become an amazing speaker. Most importantly, if we're on a team together, then I need to know that I have your full support as I'm working in this area. If I have a presentation coming up for a meeting, if I have a speech that I've agreed to give or anything where a crowd is involved, then I really need your encouragement. The more support that I have, the higher my confidence will be, and this will set me up to win.

PLAN OF ACTION

When you get nervous – Do you know what you start to feel whenever you get nervous? Is it a physical reaction (cracking voice, sweating hands, heart starts racing), or more of a mental reaction that includes negative self-talk? Whatever it is, write down what you typically feel anytime you are nervous when talking in front of people and review the tips for calming down nervousness. Try different ones, you may find that not all of them are for you, and that's ok. Focus on one or two that you believe will work, and start to make them a part of your routine when you're preparing to speak.

Practice, Practice, Practice – Are there opportunities where you could practice speaking in front of groups right now? You could start by volunteering to be the one that briefs one of the slides of a group presentation at school or at work, or you could join a volunteer organization and agree to speak in front of groups during the meetings. You could also join an organization like Toastmasters or several others that allow you to practice speaking. You can even practice speaking in front of the mirror at home by yourself if you need to. The point is to consistently be practicing and getting better. If you're able to practice speaking in front of others, be sure and tell them upfront that you need their feedback. Allow them to critique how you present your information and don't take anything that they say personally. Any feedback that you receive will be notes that you can take down to improve on.

What's your mantra? – Write down a phrase, a saying, a scripture, or some other wording that gives you peace whenever you read it. Commit this to memory. You may need to have it hanging up on your wall or on the bathroom mirror as a positive affirmation to start your mornings. The next time you are going to be speaking in front of a room of people, focus on repeating your mantra in your head. Get in the habit of repeating it anytime you feel nervous or unsure when you're getting ready to communicate.

BONUS SECTION - DELIVERING EFFECTIVE PRESENTATIONS

Ok, so I had to add a bonus section to this chapter. Public speaking is a skill that took me over 10 years of my professional career to even begin to understand, and truthfully, I'm continuing to look for ways to improve. Curing our nervousness, practicing, and having a positive mantra are all excellent practices that will lead to you portraying the image of a confident speaker. However, there is an additional skill that goes a layer deeper, and I feel it is equally as important. That skill is delivering effective presentations. We focused attention on the process and steps that it will take to become comfortable and grow in the skill of public speaking. Now I want to focus on ensuring the actual material being presented will resonate with your audience and deliver your overall message effectively. You can be someone that is incredibly comfortable in front of a crowd, but if the actual material you're speaking about isn't communicating the right message, then the presentation will be lacking something. Conversely, someone can have an amazing slide presentation with all of the colors, slide transitions, graphics, etc., and lack the confidence to bring it to life.

My goal is for you to have the ability to excel at both. The tips below apply regardless of the type of presentation you have to give or the audience:

Communicate the Bottom-Line Up Front – "BLUF"

What is the ultimate takeaway that you want people to get from your presentation? I have sat in hundreds of presentations in my engineering career, the majority of which have been heavily technical in subject matter. But I've also been in several presentations where the subject matter was more cost and schedule-oriented, where the presenter was speaking about the financial health of a program. Lastly, through years of being in the networking marketing industry, I've seen a number of presentations that were more sales-driven where the person speaking was ultimately hoping to promote and sell a product or service.

In all of these scenarios and in any type of presentation, it comes down to this for me, what is the point? What is the point the person needs to get across, and why should everyone there care to listen to it? It is critically important that you communicate this to your audience. If your presentation format is through powerpoint slides or some other program, then have what I call a "bumper sticker" or a highlighted text box on any slide where there is a point you want people to take away. An example would be in a presentation where an engineer is presenting highly technical information to a room full of finance people. There will be slides filled with words and various points of data, but on each slide, there should be a takeaway. An example would be under all of the technical jargon on a slide having a BLUF box that states:

"Widget B is currently having technical issues that could lead to a cost overage of $50,000".

Another slide could have a BLUF box that states:

"The team is currently working overtime to address the technical issues, with the goal to reduce the cost growth and pull in schedule within the next 3 weeks."

If there are no slides or visual media for the audience to look at, then the speaker/presenter will have to make key BLUF statements throughout their presentation. A BLUF statement during the same meeting with no slides might sound like this:

"I know that we've covered a lot of data here. The bottom line is this; our team has run into technical issues that have the potential to increase our product cost by $50,000. However, we are currently working overtime to address this issue to reduce cost and pull in schedule within the next 3 weeks."

The key point here is that there must be a set of takeaway points that are communicated to the audience. Your audience will be drawn directly to and will remember the BLUF statements in your presentation, and that's exactly what you want.

Anticipate and get ahead of the hard questions

We partially covered this concept in the previous pillar about the importance of practice, now we'll take it a layer deeper. There are different types of presentations. In some cases, the speaker/presenter is communicating information where there will not be a question and answer period with the audience. One example would be a preacher giving a sermon at a church or a politician giving a speech to a crowd. However, if you plan to present information where the format is one where questions can be asked, then it is very important to anticipate what those questions might be. There was a senior director that I used to brief regularly in one of my past program engineering roles. I was not only briefing him, but there would typically be over 30 other directors, department managers, and engineering leads at the meeting. One thing that he became well known for was asking tough questions. My first few presentations to him did not go well. I would go as far as to say that they didn't go well at all. I was briefing the overall engineering status of our various programs, which included how we were performing to our financial baselines and projections. It's not that I didn't know the subject matter or know my programs. It's that he would regularly throw me a curveball while I'd be talking. An example would be if I had a metric on a slide that showed we were overrunning our cost for the quarter by $100,000. I would begin briefing the slide and speaking to each number; in the middle of talking, he would stop me and ask,

"So Terrance, what is that $100,000 cost overrun about?"

I would give an answer, but that would lead to another question.

"I hear you saying there is a technical issue that led to this, but we've done this type of design before. So why are we really spending more money than expected on this?"

This would turn into what I like to call the 'snowball,' where one question leads to another one, and another, and another. If you are not careful to answer clearly and confidently, you slowly start to lose the people that you're presenting to. So, here's how to get ahead of a situation like this. When I began to do this, my presentations with that director began to improve drastically.

Study the material you're about to present, whether on slides or a presentation you'll be giving with nothing visual for the audience to look at. If there is anything in your presentation that could be perceived as bad news, then I want you to highlight it and make sure you understand everything related to that issue. Then when you're presenting, make sure to address it as soon as you get to that slide or as soon as you reach that point of your speech. You may even consider putting it in a BLUF box, as mentioned in the previous section. You want to be the one that brings it up, not someone else. This shows your audience that you're not hiding from it, and you're not trying to paint a rosy picture that isn't true. Additionally, since you've been studying the details related to the particular issue, you've already prepared yourself to be asked about it.

Confirm understanding

Has anyone ever asked you a question, and you immediately respond with an answer to which they say,

"Well, that's not actually what I was asking about."

The natural reaction when someone asks us a question is to respond swiftly. In our minds, any hesitation can come off as us being unsure of ourselves. We believe that the quick response indicates that we know what we're talking about. At least the person we're talking to will receive it that way. But this is not always the case. It is easy to react to a question too quickly and miss the core of what is being asked. I see this frequently in job interviews when a candidate is asked a question, and they fire off an answer that completely misses the mark. And it happens during presentations as well. If you're asked a question that you don't understand, then be sure and repeat the question. A way to do this is to say the following:

"So what I think you just asked me is (insert question), do I have that right?"

Now that person will either tell you that you interpreted them correctly, and you can proceed with giving them your answer. Or they're going to say that they were asking something completely different, in which case it's a good thing you asked them to repeat it. Miscommunication happens all of the time, so small practices like this one help to eliminate a lot of confusion.

If you don't know the answer, then take action or throw an assist

Sometimes despite how much you've prepared, practiced, and studied, you just won't know the answer. When you're in the moment of having to field a question that you don't know the answer to, it can be a nerve-racking experience if you don't know how to handle it. In these moments, I suggest two approaches:

1) Say that you don't have the answer, but you'll get the answer.
2) Direct the question to someone else on your team that can answer it.

Both of these approaches require a certain level of humility, to admit in front of several other people that you don't know something. But ultimately, if handled correctly, then the people watching you present will respect your honesty and professionalism. For the first approach, the key is to have a good understanding of the question and promise to follow-up with an answer. You also want to commit yourself to a timeframe that you'll provide the answer. Don't just say,

"I don't have the answer today, but I'll be sure and get back to you."

You want to say something like,

"I don't have the answer today, but as soon as we leave this meeting, I'm going to connect with my team, and I will have an answer for you within the next 24 hours."

This does two things; it holds you accountable to your commitment, and it shows the person that asked the question that you are serious about following up. The next step then obviously is to ensure you keep your word and provide them with an answer by the time that you committed to. The second approach is one that I love to do because it allows my team members to shine and takes the pressure off of me at the same time! If you are asked a question that you don't know, then throw it to someone else that can answer it. Now, this is where it is paramount to know your people, primarily their strengths and their weaknesses. Look for opportunities to toss questions to them when you can, especially if the topic is one that you're unfamiliar with. Real leaders should love to throw assists more than they love to take shots.

Avoid death by PowerPoint

We've all either given presentations this way or have witnessed when someone else does it. A slide goes up during a meeting, and the person starts reading the slide word for word. They transition to the next slide and again are repeating every word in a robotic tone. I have heard this referred to as death by PowerPoint, and trust me, it's not what you want. So how do you avoid being that person? The answer goes back to an earlier pillar that we covered; it's simply practice. See, I'm convinced that when people are reading off slides word for word, it means one thing, they aren't that comfortable with the material. Let's be honest; anyone can read a slide. But only someone that's an expert in the topics being covered in their presentation can use a slide package as a tool to drive their point home while also not relying on it. And that's how you want to be seen as an expert. A great way to practice this is to do dry runs. Look through your slide package prior to presenting it and make a note of a few key takeaway points for each slide. The points that you're going to bring up should be things that will bring more life and attention to the words you'll be showing on your slides. After all, a slide can only fit so many words and pictures on it. It's up to you to paint the picture that you want the audience to see. Run through your presentation over and over, focusing on things that you need the audience to hear. When you're practicing, make sure that you don't find yourself staring at the slides the entire time. This will force you to become familiar and comfortable with what you'll want to say.

Chapter 9 – Service

"There are few things in this life that we can control. But one thing we can control is our impact on the lives of others."

What's the fastest path to get a promotion at work? What's the best way to take your new business venture and have it impact as many people as possible? What's the most effective approach for you to be able to impact your local community? It all centers around how many people you can help. As human beings, we can be extremely selfish at times, and society supports this mindset. We want to have everything go our way. If we're not happy with our job, then we automatically think about all of the things that our coworkers or our boss do that we don't like. If we've launched a business venture and aren't receiving the level of support that we expected, then we blame our friends and family for not buying our products and not supporting our dream. Commercials that show people on vacations to exotic locations talk about how much you deserve to be there and how you deserve to treat yourself. There is marriage and relationship advice which suggests that you deserve to be happy at all times, and if you're not, then the solution is easy. Hire a divorce lawyer and leave, or break up with your significant other and go separate ways. Nevermind the fact that happiness is an emotion that can go up and down from day to day. Society would tell you to just focus on what makes you happy, because it's all about what you want.

After reading countless books on leadership development, working directly with a variety of successful leaders, and being consumed with the topic of leadership for several years, the exact opposite has proven to be true. In reality, successful people are always looking for ways to bring value to the lives of other people over their own. I want you to try an exercise. Think about the 5 people that you spend the most time hanging out with or just talking to in general. Now I want you to sit and really think about what you all spend your time talking about. How much time do those 5 people spend talking about themselves, and how much time do they spend talking about helping out other people? Maybe you all spend a lot of time talking about how each other's jobs or businesses are going and all of the moves you're planning to make this year. The new house or new car that one of you has just bought or plans to buy. Or it could be the vacation that someone else just got back from overseas to a location that you've always wanted to visit. By the way, there's absolutely nothing wrong with these conversations. I engage in these conversations often. But continue to think about those 5 people, and now ask yourself these questions:

How much time do you all spend talking about ways that you could help people that are struggling?

How often do you hear your friends celebrate someone else's business that is launching or someone else's promotion on their job?

When you all ask each other, "How are you doing?" is it a genuine question? Meaning that person really wants to know and listens intently to your answer, or is it just a gateway question that allows them to talk about their day.

Now the most important and maybe alarming question, what about you? Are your daily interactions with other people centered around you? If so, it's time to reprogram that way of thinking. In all things, the question should be how can I be of service to others. As a leader, you will be most effective when other people realize that you don't have to make everything about you. In fact, the goal should be to live life in a way where the ultimate joy comes from seeing others win. I've been to several funerals over the years, mostly for my family members and friends. Throughout the years, I noticed that every funeral had one thing in common. At each one,

I saw people share personal memories of that person, and speak about how that person helped their life in some way. In my family, there are certain people that have passed away decades ago, but there are still stories told to this day about them. That type of legacy only comes from a person dedicating their life to putting the needs of others first.

I want you to start going out of your way to help as many people as you can. Now here's the part where I'm supposed to say this – "you should help people because when you help others win, that means you're going to win!" Sorry but I'm not going to say that. Although that might be true in many circumstances, you helping other people to be successful in whatever they're pursuing can lead to you being put in similar positions to succeed. But that is ultimately not the point here. The point is to develop a servant's heart. It's an internal switch that needs to be turned on. A servant leader will help someone on their team whether other people are watching or not. A servant leader will constantly sacrifice for the betterment of his or her teammates. And a servant leader will wake up in the morning asking the question, 'Who can I help today?'. It's a rare way to think, and it goes against everything that society tells us should matter. But servant leaders are rare, and that's exactly what I want all of us to be.

Some people may feel that being a leader is about getting the recognition and the glory. But that just hasn't been my experience. I've interacted with countless teachers, sports coaches, pastors, entrepreneurs, investors, managers, chief engineers, and others throughout my life. The leaders that pour into people always have the greatest impact and are the best to be around. Develop this mindset of servant leadership, and you've taken a huge step toward becoming the leader you want to be.

TALLAHASSEE ROOTS

When the thought crosses my mind about how important it is to help others, I realize that I grew up seeing it in action constantly. The majority of my family is from Tallahassee, Florida, and by this point in the book, you've heard the city mentioned enough that I'm sure you can tell how central it is to my life story. Outside of the capitol buildings that sit in the heart of the downtown area, the two universities, and the airport (which has a total of 2 gates, A and B), it is a quiet town where you can travel from one side to the other in about 15 minutes. My parents grew up on different sides of the city but grew up attending the same church, Philadelphia Baptist Church, so their families knew each other very well. When I was growing up, we used to visit Tallahassee often. The majority of my parent's siblings and their parents lived in Tallahassee, along with countless cousins and friends. My grandparents on my dad's side were all about serving others. My grandmother Maude was a nurse at Miracle Hill Nursing Home for several years, where she cared for patients. She was also passionately referred to in our family as the "food pusher." This nickname was earned because if anyone showed up to her house after embracing you with a hug, her next question would often be,

"Baby, are you hungry? I got something for you if you need".

To which you might respond,

"Actually, I'm ok grandma. Thank you so much for offering."

To which she would reply,

"Oh, I know you need something, don't worry about it. Let me see what I can put together right quick".

The next thing you knew, after sitting in the living room for a few minutes, she'd call you to the kitchen, and she would have a full course meal laid out, with desert...oh the desert, I could write a book about her pound cake and teacakes alone, but I digress. On top of that, she'd always make sure you would leave with a plate to go. When I was in school at FAMU, there were times that I was low on money, and gourmet dinner for me meant a chicken or shrimp flavored Ramen Noodle pack that I had in the pantry. I can't count the number of times that grandma Maude would have me stop by and end up sending me on my way with bags full of food. And it wasn't just me that she did this for; she was always thinking about other people before herself. My dad's father, Fred Lee, was also a servant leader for the community and for his family. You heard a lot about him and his legacy of leadership in our earlier chapter on 'Accountability', he remains a pivotal influence on my life.

My mother's parents were my grandmother Mary Pemberton and grandfather Moses Pemberton. They raised 10 children in a 3-bedroom, 1 bathroom house on Volusia Street, less than 5 minutes from the Frenchtown area where my grandfather Fred Lee was policing. My grandmother was a loving woman, but she was also feisty. One time when I was in college we were going to church one Sunday morning. We were walking towards the steps of the church, and I grabbed for my grandmother's arm to help her up the steps. She turned to me and said with a smirk, "Boy, I don't need no help...", she then proceeded to push my hand away and walked herself up the stairs. She was 95 years old at the time by the way. To which I responded in a mild voice, "Yes, ma'am." And there was nothing mean-spirited about it at all; that was just how strong and independent she was. She also loved her family very much and was truly a giver. Similar to my grandma Maude, she would always invite me over and open up her home and her kitchen to me. She would then proceed to fix me a plate of food without me even asking. There were times when I was down to the last $10 in my account at the bank and would be trying to figure out how to make my money stretch for the next 3 days so that I could eat. I would never bring up my financial situation to them, but somehow every time I was unsure of where my next meal was coming from, if I was at my grandmother's house, then she and my uncle Junior would put a few $20 bills in my hand as I was walking out of the door. I would always tell them I didn't need it, that I was ok. But it was almost like they knew without me having to say anything. They literally saved me time and time again.

My grandfather, granddaddy Moses, as I called him, passed away when I was 9 years old. Although I was young when he passed, he left an unforgettable mark on my life. granddaddy Moses didn't have a lot of formal education or formal training; he dropped out of grade school in the 6th grade so that he could work and help take care of his family. He worked several jobs, primarily as a janitor and a dishwasher at a local restaurant. Although he never had the most money in the bank, one thing that my granddaddy did have was wisdom. He had a lot of different sayings that he used to say around us. The one that always stood out to me was when he'd say

"Boy, if you can't say nothing nice, then don't say nothing at all."

For some reason, that one stuck with me. I would hear him say it all the time, and when I was young, I didn't really know what it meant. It wasn't until I got older that I realized how wise my grandfather was and the values of respect that he was instilling in me. He believed in the power of words to build someone up or to tear them down. It's a life lesson that I've always remembered.

I also remember laughing a lot with him; he would tell jokes and always seemed to be smiling. There was a chair in the living room that he always sat in, and he always sat at the head of the dinner table in the dining room. He had a presence that I respected and admired. On the day of his funeral, I didn't go to the ceremony; maybe my parents thought it would have been too much for me to handle, since we were very close. I did end up going to the repass after the service was over; everyone was in the basement of the church. At one point, I snuck away from the table where my parents, grandmothers, uncles, and aunts were sitting. I walked up the stairs to the church sanctuary. My grandfather's casket was there in front of the pulpit, surrounded by flowers. I sat there on the front pew by myself with no one else in the sanctuary, remembering him and trying to make sense of the fact that this man who meant so much to me was now gone. I'll never forget his smile, his wisdom, and his character.

My senior year in college was an interesting time. Around this time, I was at a crossroads, I was deep into my Electrical Engineering major taking difficult classes, and it was coming close to being time to graduate. I was also heavily involved in my fraternity, was in a relationship, and was starting to try to set up interviews with companies for a potential job after graduation....while also wanting to maintain an active social life. In the midst of all of this, my grandmother Maude had developed dementia over the past few years. She was no longer living at the home off Tanner Drive that I used to visit throughout my first few years of college. She was now living in a nursing home. Coincidentally she was at Miracle Hill, the same nursing home that she had worked at for several years. The nursing home just so happened to be located a few blocks from my other grandmother's house. I would go to Miracle Hill to visit my grandma Maude often. The staff at the nursing home knew me well and took amazing care of her. I never knew what to expect, some days, I would go to visit, and grandma and I would have great conversations, laughing about funny moments from me growing up. But other days, she would either be asleep, not recognize that I was in the room, or mistake me for one of my other cousins. I would usually bring my textbooks with me, so during those times when we couldn't communicate, I would be in the room studying for an upcoming test or would be doing homework. Just being in the presence of someone who'd invested so much into me motivated me to push through and make sure I stayed focused to graduate.

After visiting grandma Maude, I would then drive around the corner to Volusia Street to my grandma Mary's house. There, my grandma and my uncle Junior, and I would sit in the living room and talk for hours. Her favorite team was the Atlanta Braves, so if she wasn't watching a Braves game, there was usually either a football or basketball game on. Uncle Junior and I would talk about our opinions on who was going to win the Super Bowl that year or what team in the NBA was going to win the title. Most important of all.... we would talk about FAMU football and the marching 100, FAMU's world famous marching band. The football team and the band were the local pride of the city, and my family was passionate about it. So we would have in-depth conversations about what FAMU needed to do to win the MEAC conference that year.

Fast forward to the fall of 2019. It was my freshman class 20-year reunion at FAMU. At this point, I was well established in my career and married with 2 children. Life was very different from when I had $10 in my bank account. After an amazing weekend of getting to see people that I hadn't seen in several years, on Sunday morning, I had some time to kill before my flight back from Tallahassee to Dallas.

I drove by three places—first, my grandfather Fred Lee's statue in Frenchtown. I got out of the rental car and stood next to the statue, looking out over the area that my grandfather used to patrol, reflecting on what his life must have been like. Next, I drove a few minutes up the road to Miracle Hill nursing home. It looked the same as when I used to visit my grandma Maude there; I thought about the times I spent in her room praying for her while studying and hoping that one day I would get the opportunity to be an engineer. Lastly, I drove around the corner and pulled up outside of my grandmother Mary's house on Volusia Street. Without expecting it, I immediately broke down into tears while sitting in the car. I didn't know what it was at the time.... but now I do. At that moment, I realized all of the people that had invested their time, love, and attention in me for so many years. My grandma Maude, grandma Mary, granddaddy Moses, and uncle Junior have all passed on from this life. All that I had sitting in the rental car that day were the memories of all of the good times we had and a heart that was full of thanks for the many sacrifices that were made for me.

There are few things in this life that we can control. But one thing we can control is our impact on the lives of others. Being a leader means constantly looking for opportunities to serve others, not to be served. You have the chance to impact someone's life forever.

THREE PILLARS OF SERVICE

START WITH YOUR CIRCLE OF INFLUENCE

Take a minute and think about people that are in your immediate circle of influence. Who do you spend at least 3 hours a week or more talking to? For many of us, this would be someone in our family, a coworker, a business partner, or a friend. Now think about your typical conversations and the topics that you all talk about. Oftentimes in our daily interactions, people will casually bring up certain things that they might be struggling with. Your friend might start talking about a recent breakup with their ex, your coworker might mention how they're really nervous about their presentation that's coming up, or your business partner may be going through a personal issue that has them feeling depressed. We can get so caught up in the routine of engaging in conversation that we often miss these clues and cries out for help that people are giving us.

Here's something to try. The next time you're talking to someone, be listening intently for areas where they might be struggling. Regardless of what that thing is that they bring up, allow your mind to brainstorm on various ways that you could help them. In many cases, the answer might be as simple as you giving your time to sit there with no distractions and listen to them pour their heart out. Many people go through life holding their pain inside, even from their closest friends and family members. I know because I've done this. Most of the time, this is because they don't feel like being a burden on anyone else, and they might feel like no one will care. So one way that you can be of service is simply to offer a safe space for that person to vent. In other cases, your help might require much more. It may be that someone in your circle lacks the financial means to take care of a dire situation in their personal life, and you're in a position to help them. Maybe someone on your team at work is struggling with their current project because it's not in their area of expertise, and that area happens to be your strength. Or maybe you have a family member or friend that is a single parent raising children, working extremely hard to provide and to guide them through life. You may have the unique opportunity to partner with that parent to help stand in the gap and share your life experiences and wisdom with those children as a mentor. The point here is to begin to listen and think about the needs of others first.

By the way, you must view any act of service as a one-way transaction. Meaning you should be helping this person with no expectation of anything in return. This definitely goes against the quid pro quo, help me, and I'll help you mentality that prevails in our world. However, this is the best form of giving. It comes when you know that you are doing something because you genuinely want to help somebody. When it isn't forced, isn't planned, and there is no gain attached to it. When help is given under these circumstances, then you know that your intentions are pure. So, look for ways that you can provide this type of selfless help to people in your circle of influence. As you transition into this new mindset, you'll notice your thought patterns will begin to change. As a leader, this is a skill that is often overlooked, but it's something that can transform the culture of a team. When your team knows that you are not just about helping yourself, then they will fight for you because ultimately, they know you'll fight for them.

SERVE WHEN NOBODY IS WATCHING

Now, this part of the book might get me in a little trouble, but I just feel like it's necessary. If it seems like I'm speaking to you here, then I can ensure you that my intent is not to offend (I've been guilty in the past of the examples I'm going to give below too), my intent is simply the following:

1) Change your perspective of what it means to genuinely help someone.
2) Force us to look in the mirror to evaluate our true intentions for why we're serving people.

When I'm on social media, I see this every day, and you probably have too. Posts with long captions saying something like,

"Wow, I feel so blessed to have served for 2 hours at the homeless shelter today! It feels so good to help others! #blessed #service (insert 30 other hashtags)."

Or the Happy Valentine's Day, Happy Anniversary, Happy Birthday posts on social media from one significant other to another. In the post, you'll typically see pictures of everything the person did for that other person, including a long post about love and, of course, a.... #blessed (insert 30 other hashtags). Here's the thing, post whatever and however you want to on your pages. I am in no position to judge anyone about anything, and as I said, I have posted similar things before. I'm simply using that as an illustration of how it feels at times that our society has become a culture of searching for likes. If we're truly serving people, then our motive should ultimately be to help them, right? It really doesn't matter if anybody else ever knows about it. It doesn't even matter if the person that we helped ever says thank you. What matters is the heart behind the help. So, what are your motives? If your motive is true service, then your motives are in the right place and will likely be very clear to other people that are around you. If we're honest about it, when people are helping others, and they want credit for it, it's usually pretty obvious. Just think about this, if an opportunity came up for you to speak to a group of kids, to be a mentor, to feed the homeless, to serve at your local church, would you do any of those things if there was never a camera on you and nobody ever wrote about it? Really sit in that question and dwell on it. This will inform you of where the intentions in your heart truly lie.

So, am I saying to never post a picture on social media of you helping other people, or to never tell your loved ones that you love them on social media? That's not the point of what I'm saying. The point is to check your heart and to check your intentions. If your post is really about the fact that you want to share the joy that you feel from helping someone or the joy that your significant other gives you, then that is great. If that's the case, then it shouldn't matter if your post gets a single like or comment because that's not your intention.

One of my favorite things to do at this point in life is random acts of kindness for people in my circle as well as for complete strangers. I don't know how to explain it, but there's a deep satisfaction that I have from knowing that one action from me could have a positive impact on that person's life. Who cares if anyone else sees it? You helped where you could, and that made someone else's life a little easier that day. That's all that matters.

Here are a few quick ideas for ways that you can choose to serve, many of which are incredibly easy to do:

- Be sure to always have some physical currency on you. Make it a routine to give money, food or clothing to any homeless people that you see in your area.
- Sign up to serve at a local homeless shelter or soup kitchen.
- Drop off food at a local food donation center.
- When you're in a drive-thru line, tell the cashier that you would like to pay for the person's food behind you.
- If you're eating at a restaurant and you can afford to do so, leave the waiter or waitress a substantial tip beyond the recommended 20-25%.
- If someone that you know has a son or daughter that is misguided and in need of guidance, offer to be a mentor for them.
- If you see trash in your neighbor's yard, pick it up for them and don't tell them that you did it.
- When you've paid the bill at a restaurant you're eating at, clean up the table so that the waiter or waitress doesn't have to.

The acts listed above are not sexy or flashy, and that's the point. I believe this is the attitude of a true leader, being willing to help people with their problems even when nobody else will know and when you know that you will never get the credit. So now that we've covered that, if you could please copy and paste this pillar and share it on your Instagram, Facebook, Twitter, Snapchat, and all other platforms, I would greatly appreciate it because I am #blessed #grateful #thankful!! I'm kidding folks...

BUILD ON POTENTIAL

Think of someone in your life that believed in you at some point. It could have been a parent, a family member, teacher, coach, or mentor. Regardless of who it is, everyone has potential that can be brought out of them given the right circumstances. As a manager, when I'm talking to my team members about their career goals and current assignments, I'm always thinking about their potential for the future. What goals are they trying to achieve in their career? What skills do they need to develop in order to get there? How can I help them to build those skills? A key skill to develop as a leader is the ability to study people. When someone is talking to you about their goals, their dreams, and what they enjoy doing, you have to listen with the intent to learn. You'll notice subtle things. When they start talking about a particular project they're working on, their face will light up, or their voice inflection will increase, or the opposite will happen. Either one is a clue to help you understand what motivates that person. Equally as important, you will know what prevents them from being motivated. Couple that with observations about them that you're able to make as you work together. Over time you start to pick up on things that people are good at.

Based on those observations and the person's goals, you might think this person has the potential to be a great team lead or an individual contributor that is a subject matter expert in their field. They may interact well with kids and students, so maybe they have the potential to be a great teacher or mentor. Maybe that person has a passion for music or the arts, but everyone has always told them to avoid being a 'starving artist.' You may be able to help pull the potential out of that person and change their perspective. When you can discover what motivates people and marry that with their potential, then you have something to build on. As a leader, this ends up making the entire team dynamic better. Imagine a team where everyone in the room is aware of what they're good at, everyone has their niche,' and everyone is growing. On top of that, imagine that everyone on the team knows that the leader believes in them and sees the potential in them. Now you have a powerful, high-performing team in place.

WHAT INTROVERTS WISH EXTROVERTS KNEW

As an introvert, I love to help other people. Of course no two people are completely the same, but in general because introversion is often linked to empathy, I naturally think about the feelings of other people first. For this reason, the concept of servant leadership, putting the needs of the team above my own is one that I easily can identify with. This makes me an optimal candidate for leadership positions, as I will be quick to consider the needs of everyone and quick to seek opportunities to help other people.

PLAN OF ACTION

Start with your circle of influence

Write down 1-3 names of people in your immediate circle of friends, family, co-workers, or business associates that you know are struggling with something personally or professionally right now. If you can't think of anyone, then make up your mind that you're going to do something for a stranger. Now write down at least one thing that you can do right now to help them. This does not have to be a grand gesture; it can be something small. Lastly, commit to the day and time that you're going to do it. My suggestion would be to go do it today while it is fresh on your mind. After all, there's no day like today to help someone out.

Serve when nobody is watching

Now, here's the difficult part for some. When you help the person or people that you wrote down above, I don't want you to post it on any form of social media or let anyone know about it. It will be strictly between you and the people that you're helping. Give yourself a timeframe, and I can't tell what that exact timeframe will be because you have to decide for yourself. Maybe you'll say that for the next 6 months, you won't post about any situations where you've helped the less fortunate, or instead of posting about something you did for your significant other's birthday, you'll choose to live in the moment with them instead of picking up your phone. What will most likely happen (which is what has happened with me) is that you'll begin to question yourself anytime you're about to post on social media. You'll begin to think, "Am I posting this because I want recognition? Because I want likes?" Eventually, you'll notice that your approach to helping others will change. Remember, any acts of service are for others; it's not about your like count going up.

Build On Potential

Think about and write down 1-3 people that you interact with frequently that you feel have untapped potential. Next, write down what you feel their unique gift is. The key here is for it to be unique; when you think of this person, there should be something that separates them from other members of your team. Now begin to think about what you can do as a leader to help them build on that potential. It could be as simple as talking to them about it, mentoring them through it, or connecting them with someone else that can mentor them through it. You will be surprised how many people don't realize the level of their gifts and abilities until some- one else shows them.

CHAPTER 10 – EFFORT

"I can't promise that you'll accomplish everything that you ever set out to do, but I can promise that if you make it a habit to ALWAYS do your best at everything you set out to do, that decision alone will change your life."

What makes some people successful, while other people seem to consistently struggle to reach their goals? Michael Jordan, an introvert by the way, is highly regarded by many as the best basketball player of all time. I grew up in the '90s, so this is no argument for me, although I'm always open to entertain a debate for the late Kobe Bryant, aka Black Mamba. Some would say that no matter how many shots a person practiced in a basketball gym over a period of years, their skill would never end up reaching the level of Michael Jordan. Anyone that knows his story knows that Michael Jordan's work ethic and competitiveness were on a level that has probably never been seen in all of sports. Despite the thousands of shots that Jordan practiced for years and years, some would still conclude that he was destined for the greatness he achieved and had a natural athletic ability that most people would just never be able to match. If you were to decide today that you want to be the next Michael Jordan, and you committed to putting in the hours necessary to accomplish that goal, guess what? There's a good chance that it might not happen. In fact, about 3 out of every 10,000 high school senior basketball players end up getting drafted by a professional NBA team, about 0.03 percent. Among the ones who make it to the league, those that will impact the game at the level of a Michael Jordan are incredibly slim.

The reality is that every time someone writes down a goal and starts putting in the work toward that goal, they still might not meet it. When I was in college, I started the practice of writing my goals down on paper, I actually can't remember why I started doing it, but it's been a common thing for me ever since. In my life, I haven't accomplished every single goal that I've written down; there are many that I have but also several that I have not. So what does someone have to do to achieve his or her goals? There have been countless books written around this very topic, I know because I've read a lot of them. After now living through different phases of life, wins, and losses, equal amounts of excitement and disappointment, the answer has become quite simple. The only thing that we can control is our effort.

Are some people put in positions to win without having to work hard? Absolutely. Some kids are born into a family where their parents have social connections with people at the college that they'll want to attend one day, so they're guaranteed to get in. Some people decide to start a business and are given a $100,000 investment from a family member to get started. Some people even win the lottery and become millionaires overnight. These things do happen, but the reality is those things are completely outside of a person's control. What you can always control is your effort. Let's be honest for a minute. Whenever you've set a goal to get something accomplished in your life, have you always given 100% of yourself to make sure it gets done? For those of you reading this book that can answer yes to that question, congratulations. For those of you that have flaws and have made mistakes like me, you can probably identify with having a dream but not always doing what it took to make that dream come true. I can't promise that you'll accomplish everything that you ever set out to do, but I can promise that if you make it a habit to ALWAYS do your best at everything you do, that decision alone will change your life.

This is great news for introverts because this doesn't require you to become someone that you're not. Whatever your position is on any team and in any situation, you can always control your effort. Coincidentally, people that work hard often recognize other people that operate the same way. I can't tell you how many people I've encountered in my career that weren't necessarily the top engineer on a team but were well respected by all levels of leadership for their work ethic. As a manager, I've reviewed hundreds of resumes and have led or participated in a number of candidate interviews. There are a lot of people that look great on paper, where you read their resume and are convinced this person is a superstar. A high-grade point average and a solid undergraduate degree from a good school are great and are things that get most people's attention upon first glance at a resume. What I've learned is that for me, if I'm looking to build a strong team at work or in business, the formula is very simple. I always look to team up with people that have high standards for their work and are passionate about meeting those standards. Those things are hard to see on a resume because it speaks more to the core of who the person is. There are people with several degrees from multiple universities and impressive grade point averages that may completely fold when put into a high-pressure situation. Meanwhile, another person's grade point average may be several points below the others, but that person is ambitious, genuine, and ready to work. I will take the second person every time; it's to a point now where I've developed a pretty good sense for who is who. As a leader, the attitude to have is to always be the hardest worker in the room. It's the one thing that we can always control, and when it's done consistently, people notice and respect it. So, if you have a dream, a goal, or a desire that drives you, then you owe it to yourself to commit 100% to it.

Unfortunately, this is a lesson that I've learned on more than one occasion. I've thrown away several opportunities in my life due to my lack of effort and not appreciating what I'd been blessed with at the time. My hope is that if you look in the mirror and feel like you haven't been trying, haven't been giving your all, and want to give up on the goals you've been pursuing that you would take a lesson and gain inspiration from these stories. I had to learn the importance of this leadership principle the hard way, by hitting bottom. Ultimately the sole purpose of this book is to help you reach your full potential, and oftentimes experience is the best teacher. So here goes....

FROM FREE COLLEGE TO 10 YEARS OF STUDENT LOAN DEBT

In May 2000, when I finished my second semester at Florida A&M University, I went from having a scholarship that would pay 100% of the cost for my undergraduate college degree to being responsible for paying $78,000 in tuition, fees, room, and board over the next 3 years. Yeah, I know. Let that sink in for a minute. I didn't know it at the time, but one four-month semester of not being focused would cost me for several years.

In high school, I was a basketball player and had been since I was 7 years old. I always felt that I would get a full basketball scholarship to a big division 1 school like North Carolina, Duke, or Michigan. I was a huge Fab Five fan, so Chris Webber, Jalen Rose, Juwan Howard, Jimmy King, and Ray Jackson were guys that I looked up to when they were playing at the University of Michigan. The summer before my senior year of high school I had planned to attend several basketball camps where college scouts would be there looking for recruits. My AAU coach at the time had us playing in local tournaments between Dallas, Houston, and Oklahoma that summer. However, when it was time to travel to the big tournaments (the Las Vegas and Atlanta tournaments were the largest showcases for high school players at the time), only a few players from our AAU team were selected to travel. I was one of the guys that didn't get selected; as a result of that, I missed a lot of the major summer tournaments, which meant I missed getting a lot of exposure with the college scouts. At the time, I was getting interest and a few recruiting letters from some small division 1 schools and division 3 schools in Texas. But none were from schools I wanted to attend.

Needless to say, my dream of being the next NBA star was quickly starting to fade, and it was time to figure out the next steps for my life.

One night in the spring of 1999, my mom had attended a scholarship dinner in Dallas that was hosted by alumni of Florida A&M and university president Dr. Frederick Humphries. At that dinner, the university was giving out scholarships to high school seniors in the Dallas/Fort Worth area. When my mom mentioned going to the dinner, I didn't think much of it at the time; I certainly didn't expect to get anything. Well, later that night, my mom came home and told me that I'd received a full academic scholarship offer to attend FAMU in the fall. I had worked very hard between my sophomore and senior years, taking advanced classes and performed well on the SAT test. So, it felt like all of that work had paid off. It was one of the happiest days of my life.

I'd grown up around FAMU because the majority of my extended family lived in Tallahassee, so I was very familiar with the school and with the area. I arrived on campus in the fall of 1999, young, excited, and ready for college life. I started making friends within my first few weeks on campus. I was meeting people from all over the country: students from Florida, Atlanta, Detroit, Chicago, California, New York, Philadelphia, St Louis, and others. I ended up meeting several people that were from Texas like me. For a major, I chose Electrical Engineering, I had loved math and science since I was a kid, so the thought of one day being an engineer was special for me. That first semester as a freshman, I had 16 credit hours of classes on my schedule. For those reading this that may not be aware, a lot of students lose their minds during their first semester in college. For parents, their worst nightmare is that their kid will go to college and not know how to handle their newly found freedom. They'll get to campus, party every day, flunk out of their classes and end up coming back home. That first semester I would say I was able to balance my responsibilities while still managing to have some fun. I was there on the Distinguished Scholarship Award and kept reminding myself that I was there to take care of my business and graduate in 4 years. So, I studied, spent a lot of time at the library, and for the most part, stayed focused. When I wasn't studying, I was usually on the Set, located at the center of campus where all the students would hang out, or with my friends in the dorm or going to CPA, The Moon or The Garden, all well known Tallahassee clubs at the time. It ended up being a great semester. I had made new friends, managed to meet a new girlfriend, and also finished with a 3.6 GPA. After the semester, I went back to Dallas for the winter break and couldn't wait to show my parents my grades. They were happy for me, and it was a good feeling. After relaxing for a few weeks with my family and catching up with my Dallas friends, it was time to head back to Tallahassee for the spring. But my mentality had changed somewhat. I had gotten a 3.6 GPA in the fall, so obviously, I had figured this college thing out. Here I thought that my college courses would be so much harder than high school, and I still had an A average like I was used to. So, what could go wrong?

For the spring 2000 semester, I only signed up for 12 credit hours; in my mind, I'd already gotten a 3.6 GPA, and that was with 16 credit hours. So, I would take fewer hours; that way, I could have a little more fun that semester and wouldn't have to stress as much. Besides...I'd earned the right to, because I'd gotten a 3.6 GPA (see how I keep bringing that up). Classes started that spring, and it was great to be back in town. I started hanging out just about every day, either with my friends or with my girlfriend at the time. While my roommate used to stay in his room and study for his upcoming tests, I would usually be out somewhere. The first semester I made it a rule to not go out much during the week that I had any type of quiz or exam. Now during the second semester, I would be at the club until 2am, then wake up to take an exam at 8 in the morning. I even had a Saturday morning Chemistry Lab because it was the only timeslot available. Talk about a bad idea. I missed several labs. When I did attend, I was usually too sleepy from hanging out the night before to pay attention. I also had a Calculus II class that was rough. I'd gotten an A+ in Calculus in my first semester, so I'd assumed that Calculus II wouldn't be that different, man, was I wrong. Even with it being a difficult class, looking back, if I would have put the focus and time into it, I would have been fine. But that's just not where my head was at that point. My focus had shifted. I was living my best life, having fun and enjoying my freedom. Well, that semester came to an end, and I got my grades. My overall GPA had dropped below 3.0, the minimum requirement to keep the DSA scholarship was a 3.0. Shortly after receiving my grades, I got an email from the university stating that I'd lost my full scholarship. I hadn't even made it to my sophomore year.

Let me breakdown the impact of that one semester. The rough cost of tuition, fees, room, and board at FAMU for an out-of-state student at the time was around $26,000 per year. Since I'd lost my scholarship, I would now have to figure out how to cover the cost of college. Assuming I'd be there for 3 more years, that was around $78,000. I applied for financial aid, got a job at Eckerd drug store, where I started working part-time, and applied for every scholarship I could find. I was blessed to get 2 partial scholarships, which was a huge help. Between getting approved for partial financial aid, money from my job, and the partial scholarships, I was able to cover the majority of my tuition and living expenses through to graduation. In the end, when I left Tallahassee after my senior year, I owed around $17,000 in student loans. This amount was far less than a lot of my classmates that I knew were paying back, but if I'd kept my scholarship, it would have been $0! I deferred making any student loan payments until 2008, which was a few years into my first engineering job that I'd started in June 2005. Of course, I was only making minimum payments to start. It took me until 2015 to pay my loan off in full.

So essentially, one four-month semester in the spring of 2000 created a financial debt that took me 7 years to pay off. I still have a copy of my report card from that semester in a picture frame, with a note from my dad where he simply wrote '3.6 GPA first semester' as a reminder. I keep that frame, and anytime I look at it, I remember that I must always do my best in all things that I do. I'll never settle for anything else again.

STUDENT OF THE YEAR

In the 7th grade, I received the student of the year award at our school, Martha Brown middle school in Rochester. The award was given to the student that had the highest grade point average for his or her class. Any student that got the award would be called into the principal's office, where they would receive a certificate and take a picture. From there, the picture would be placed in a glass case in the entryway to the school, where everyone walking in and out could see it. There was also an announcement over the PA system the morning that the award was given out, where the recipient's name was called out for the entire school to hear. It really was a big deal as the school had a lot of students, so it was something that any student should have been proud of. Well, not me. School came fairly easy to me at the time; it wasn't unusual for me to get straight A's or all A's and one B+ on my report cards. So, I received the award, which of course, made my parents proud. But by the time I got to 8th grade, being the smart kid wasn't exactly cool. With some of my friends and classmates, I was viewed as the nerd or the teacher's pet. Lunchtime in the cafeteria is really when the jokes and insults would fly. I would be joked on for always being in my books. I would defend myself with any response that I could find, but usually, the response was pretty weak and not received well. Also, now being into girls and wanting to get their attention, showing off your report card was definitely not going to get it done. At the time, girls were more into the boys that were making jokes in class and skipping school. Couple that with the fact that I was a little socially awkward and had started getting pimples, I felt like I didn't have a chance.

In my mind, the only thing that I really had in my favor was basketball and the fact I was one of the stars on the team. That allowed me to at least get noticed at some level. But I grew tired of the jokes that came with being what was perceived as a nerd. I wanted to fit in, to be cool, to be liked. So, one day in the spring of my 8th grade year, as I was taking a math test, I purposely started marking the wrong answers on several multiple-choice questions. I remember vividly because it was a test that I could've got a 100% on. When I got the results back, I could tell my teacher was surprised and with good reason. Well, I didn't stop there. I continued doing this in a few of my other classes as well through to the end of the year. Eventually, the summer came, and it was time to prepare to go to high school as a freshman. I would be at Minerva Deland, which was a freshman-only school in the Rochester suburb of Fairport. On my first day there, I knew things were different. We were in high school now, and the conversations had changed. Guys were talking about going over to girls' houses when their parents weren't home. A friend of a friend of mine showed me a bag of marijuana for the first time. And there would regularly be confrontations that turned into fights in the school hallway, usually two guys fighting over a girl. I was being exposed to more and seeing more. At the same time, I was also changing. My voice had evolved into a deep baritone; I was lifting weights daily and had grown some facial hair. People that saw me would oftentimes think I was a senior.

I started to feel grown; I had left my nerdy middle school persona behind me and was ready to recreate myself. So, I continued to not do well in school on purpose. I actually didn't do bad; I just didn't perform anywhere near what my capability was. My plan was to make my grades just good enough so that I could get by and not have any issues with my parents. But they noticed the difference. My dad would regularly call me out on it, on how I was not doing my best, and he knew I could do better. And he was absolutely right. At the time, I was more concerned with picking the right Karl Kani outfit and fresh shoes to impress the girls at my school that day. Or concerned with cracking jokes in the classroom with my friends, while the teacher proceeded to send one of us to the principal's office. Within a year, I had gone from being sent to the principal's office for an award to being sent there for punishment.

When we left Rochester in 1996 for Dallas, I started my sophomore year at Shepton High School and was able to get my grades back on track. Although I was definitely a different person by this point, not the straight and narrow kid that I was before, I at least was back to performing well in school. Looking back on that time between 8th and 9th grade when I made the decision that I made, I wish I had been strong enough to be different. This is why I believe mentoring is so important. There comes a time when a child's primary influence transitions from being their parents or parent, to being their friend groups. When that happens, not all kids are comfortable with being viewed as different because peer pressure and the need to fit in socially are very real. Regardless of where you are in your life, please don't make the mistake that I did. Dare to be different and dare to stand out. Most people in this life don't put forth a strong effort in the things they do, and for that reason, you can stand out from the crowd when you do. Always do your best, and never worry about what anyone else thinks about it.

THREE PILLARS OF EFFORT

MASTER YOUR CRAFT

One of the hardest things to do in all sports is to hit a baseball, to be more specific, a curveball that is traveling at 90 miles per hour or higher. Let's say you decided to master the art of hitting a baseball, and you planned to devote time to getting better at it. You schedule time at a local batting cage for a few hours a week and start going consistently. Your goal is to swing at over 1,000 curveballs, with the thought being that after you do this that many times you will have mastered it. You start going to the batting cage every day, and after several weeks you've swung at more than 1,000 curveballs. Have you improved? Have you mastered it? Well, the answer is that it depends. If this is your first time ever playing baseball, then you might have just swung at 1,000 curveballs and had terrible form while doing it. One of the most important factors in being a great hitter in baseball is your form; without proper form, a batter will have no chance against a good pitcher. What would it feel like to put countless hours into mastering something and at the end of that time feel like you haven't made any progress? Frustrating and disheartening, I would think.

To begin the process of mastering your craft, which is critical to your ability to do your best, you have to start with learning the basics first. So if I'm trying to learn how to hit a baseball, I should probably think about hiring a batting coach. Or maybe start studying professional baseball players during games and paying attention to how they hold and swing the bat. I could even go on YouTube and do a video search for "How to hit a curveball." The point is to study and learn the correct form, then start to swing. As a leader, when you enter a new situation and are about to start leading a team, the first job is to take in as much information as possible. If you're about to lead a new business venture or are starting a new leadership role at a company, there are a few steps that will help the journey to you mastering your craft:

1) Find the person on your team that is the most knowledgeable about the task that has to be done. Build a relationship with them and ask questions.
2) Study as much material about the project as possible.
3) Start to execute (swing) and adjust course along the way.

I've heard various perspectives about the 'dive in head first' approach. This assumes that true learning in a new role is accomplished when the individual isn't consumed with hours of training and onboarding discussions but instead starts performing their new task right away. In environments where things are very fast-paced, this can sometimes be the approach that is taken. However, even when leading teams in environments like that, the steps still apply. If you don't have a mentor that can share their experiences with you, and if you aren't armed with information about what you need to do to be successful as a leader of your team, then that is starting off with bad form. When you start with a good foundation, you're now preparing yourself to win, regardless of what the project or task you're leading is.

Now, in the beginning, you're probably going to swing and miss a lot; you're new at this, so there is no shame in that. Maybe your first time giving a presentation to the team, things won't go 100% as planned, or the first decision you make causes something to now be late that wasn't before. The key is to keep learning and adjusting. Baseball players change up their stance depending on the pitcher they are facing and might change their stance completely if something else starts working for them. This is what mastering your craft looks like. The best leaders are constantly evolving, growing, failing, recovering, and learning. Next thing you know, you'll find yourself confidently leading team discussions and communicating the vision for where the team is going at the meetings that you used to be nervous about running. As a student, you'll be proposing and implementing effective solutions to your teammates in that group project that you were shying away from being the team lead for. It will take time, but eventually, you'll start to see the difference.

SET MEASURABLE AND ATTAINABLE GOALS FOR YOURSELF

How do you plan to become a better leader? Or, if you've never been in a leadership position before, how do you plan to prepare yourself for the day when you can take on a leadership role? What's your goal, and what's your plan? Many people talk a lot about what they plan to do. Whenever I hear someone talk about a business they plan to start or the new job they're going to get, I automatically think the following:

Ok, that's great, so what is your execution plan to get there? Who are your mentors or coaches that will help get you to reach that goal? What is the target date to accomplish this? If it's a business, what is the monthly sales target and break-even point for your initial investment? If your goal is to be a manager or other type of leader at your job, when do you plan to apply for the role, and what would success look like for you if you were to get it?

Earlier in the introduction for this chapter, I talked about how I started to write down my goals. In my late 20's I set several aggressive goals for myself. Looking back, it's interesting because a lot of the goals that I wrote down at the time never came to fruition, but some of them did. I wrote spiritual, mental, financial, and emotional/relationship goals. So around that time in my life, my goals for a year looked something like this:

- Join a church and start reading the bible more.
- Read 20 books a year.
- Earn as much money in my networking marketing business as I was making at my 9 to 5 job, and get a paid for BMW from the network marketing company.
- Get married and start a family.

That was around 10 years ago.

Well, I didn't achieve all of those goals, but I did achieve some. I got married in 2013, my wife and I have been married for 7 years and have 2 children. We are also members of a local church in Prosper, Texas. On the bible reading goal, I had to get more specific, because what does it mean to make a goal that says I will do something "more"? Does more mean once a day, once a week, once a month? Recently I have found a good rhythm that works for me in this area, but I had to get specific with that goal first. On reading, I have met my goal of reading 20 books per year most years. Some years I read less, like in 2020 when I spent most of my time writing this book, and now in 2021 as I'll be spending increased time publishing and marketing it. I never reached the income goal that I had for my network marketing business, although I was able to build a team of over 250 people in my downline and make significant income that helped supplement my 9 to 5 job. Not bad, considering that in my first networking marketing company (the one I talked about in the earlier chapter with Cedrick), I didn't recruit a single person. I also don't drive a BMW, and the funny thing is now that I can afford one, I have no desire to have one. I'm perfectly ok driving around my used Nissan Altima that is paid off in full.

So I didn't achieve every single goal that I penned down on paper 10 years ago, but my life has progressed in an incredible way. And ultimately, that's all that we can ask for. A close family friend Celeste Barnes once said that if you shoot for the moon, you'll at least land among the stars. Goals allow us the freedom to dream, and putting those dreams down on paper begins to make them real. But execution and application of everything you've learned in order to achieve those goals are key. Simply writing something down means nothing if you don't plan to do something about it. However, research has shown that there is power in writing things down. There's something that happens internally when you write down your goals, so I'm a huge believer in it. Another important note is that if you're going to do your best, then you have to know the exact goal that you're trying to hit. That is why a key to setting goals is to make them clear and measurable. You might be reading this book with the goal being, I want to become a better leader. But what does that mean? Here's a clearly defined and measurable goal;

"I will write down at least one idea that I can bring up in my team's meeting by (insert date), and I will give an effective presentation about (insert topic) at work by (insert date)."

That is measurable and attainable, which means you can now devote your focus to making those things happen. And if you don't hit your goals in the timeframe that you originally gave yourself, don't beat yourself up about it. Don't get me wrong, you should hold yourself accountable, and that's why it's important to write it down. But if your suspense date for the goal passes, then cross that date out and write another one. Eventually, you will find that setting goals will become a habit, and you'll be amazed as you start to see yourself achieving them.

HAVE SOMEONE TO HOLD YOU ACCOUNTABLE

Something that will undoubtedly help you during your leadership journey is to have somebody in your corner that is there to hold you accountable, an accountability partner. Whatever you are trying to achieve, it is great to have frequent conversations with someone who is either trying to do the same thing or has an interest in seeing you be successful at what it is that you're pursuing. When someone wants to improve their grade for a class in school, lose weight, eat healthier, get a promotion, or any type of self-improvement, this is hard to do alone. Don't get me wrong, there is power in setting your mind on the achievement of a goal, then taking that goal from your mind onto paper, as mentioned in the previous pillar. But now that you have committed to putting in the work and have written down your goal, the last step is to find someone or a group that will hold you accountable to achieving it. Another person will always see things about you that you just don't see. For example, your goal could be to improve in the area of public speaking. A natural tendency might be to practice your speech or presentation to yourself at home, work on adjusting the delivery of it and continue to practice. These are good things to do but should not be the only approach.

Whenever you want to master a new skill, and you've decided to write it down as a measurable goal for yourself, the next thought should be 'who do I know that can help me.' This can be a different thought process for many people, in particular, many introverts that might tend to keep smaller circles of friends and don't naturally reach out to others for help. So what would be the right approach in this case? If you've made it the goal that you want to improve your public speaking skills in order to deliver a top-notch presentation that is coming up within the next week, then try to think of a person you know that could help you with that. Who is the best speaker that you know personally? Maybe you ask that person if you could practice a presentation for them and receive honest feedback. You might be surprised, but most people react positively when someone asks for their help. People typically like to be seen as an expert in their subject area, so when you ask someone for help, you're actually complimenting them. Of course, everyone is not giving in this way, but in my experience, I've found that many people are. If you're comfortable enough with that person, you can use the term 'accountability partner' or mentor with them. You basically want to communicate that you are passionate about improving in a specific area, and you would appreciate any help that they can offer.

Once you have a partner in place, you'll start to notice the difference. Assuming it's a good partner, they will open your eyes to constructive criticism that you can build on. Be careful to not get offended when they point out flaws, things for you to change, or for you to stop doing altogether. Trust me, honest feedback is what you want here. When you are trying to improve as a leader, you do not want 'yes men' or 'yes women' in your corner that will agree with everything that you say. You need some-one that is going to keep it real with you, the good and the bad. It will most likely be things that you never thought about yourself. This doesn't just apply to criticism; the partner will also notice positive qualities about you that you never saw. Observations like this will help to boost your confidence and will keep you going when you feel like giving up.

By the way, my natural tendency is to not seek out accountability partners. I'm analytical, a deep thinker, and a problem solver. So when I'm faced with a new challenge, I automatically start trying to solve it myself. I will say that over the past 5 years, I've been working on this and have made a lot of progress. When I make a new goal for myself, my mind now thinks, "Who do I know that is good at that?". Recently my wife and I started discussing investing in a vacation home that we could also post on Air BnB as a short-term rental property. Although I've stayed in an Air BnB before as a guest, I don't know anything about running one as a host. So, one of the first things I did was reached out to a cousin of mine that is currently hosting properties on Air BnB and asked him tons of questions. Now, if I decide to proceed with the investment, I have someone in place that is already doing it and can help hold me accountable to make sure I'm approaching it correctly. This beats the alternative of making a decision with no prior knowledge or experience in what I'm doing. You make life so much easier on yourself when you have someone else that is familiar with your goal and is invested enough in you to help you meet it.

WHAT INTROVERTS WISH EXTROVERTS KNEW

As an introvert, I can oftentimes be extremely detailed and calculated. Where you might be quick to jump to a decision or quick to take action, I am likely thinking over every possible scenario and outcome that could happen. This can lead to my being able to set very clearly defined goals, and having a clear approach for how to meet them. I may not talk as loudly as you, the extrovert, does about your aspirations and dreams, but this does not mean that my work ethic, my passion and my ambition is any less than yours.

Plan of Action

Master your craft - What would you like to become great at? It could be something that you've been working on or something you haven't even started. Whatever it is, write it down. Then I want you to commit to giving consistent and dedicated focus to it. So next, write down the amount of time that it will take to begin to master it. If you want to be a better speaker, will you need to practice speaking once a week, once a day? Should this be done over a period of 6 months, a year? An example for me was that at the start of 2020, I decided I was going to write this book. But it didn't become real until I started to actually do it almost midway through the year and continue writing it consistently. My goal was simple, to write at least one page per day and have the book done by the end of the year. Well, I didn't quite get there, but I was close. The first draft of this book was completed by the end of January 2021, and sent to my editor. So whatever you hope to accomplish, commit to putting in the time it will take to master it because it won't happen overnight.

Set measurable and attainable goals for yourself – Once you've written down the thing that you hope to improve on, now it's time to create actionable steps for how you will achieve it. Back to the book example, me saying at the start of 2020

"I want to write a book"

doesn't really mean much. But saying;

"I will write at least one page of my book every day, will be complete with the full manuscript by the end of December 2020, send that manuscript to an editor and

start working on the cover for the book in January 2021. I will spend February 2021 putting together my marketing plan for the book and networking with other authors. Also, by February 2021, I will start building up a buzz for the book prior to its release date in the summer of 2021".

That means something entirely different. Your next step is to write down the steps and the timeline needed to achieve your goal. Put the steps up on the wall in your closet, on the mirror in the bathroom, or in the office, preferably somewhere that you will physically be at some point of every day. This will serve as a constant reminder of where it is that you're trying to go.

Have someone to hold you accountable

Now that you have your sights set on a goal and have written down the plan for how you will get there, it's time to think about an accountability partner. When you have someone that you can share your dreams and goals with, they can be there to encourage you when you feel like giving up and can hold you accountable when you're not living up to your potential. Again, you don't want this to be a person that always agrees with everything you say or that has a problem confronting you. You need someone that can tell you the truth in love. If you have a person like that, then I want you to write their name down and give them a call or text. Tell them you want to meet up somewhere to talk. During that conversation, tell them what it is that you're trying to do and accomplish, and that you need them to hold you accountable. Another avenue to consider is professional coaching. There are a number of coaches available to help you through a variety of topics, whether it be professional goals, entrepreneurial goals, or personal ones. If you do decide to go the route of pursuing a professional coach, make sure it is someone that you are comfortable with and someone that has experience helping people in your specific area of need. For the record, I recently decided to hire a professional coach for my business, and it's one of the best decisions I've made.

CONCLUSION

O ne of my favorite poems is by Robert Frost, it is titled "The Road Not Taken." The poem speaks about a traveler that approaches two roads in the woods that are headed in different directions. In this poem, the roads are metaphorical, as the illustration is used to represent a choice in life that the traveler has to make. It concludes with the following:

"Two roads diverged in a wood, and I...

I took the one less traveled by,

And that has made all the difference."

Choosing to be a leader as an introvert is a road that is not traveled by many. You will make mistakes, you will upset some people, you will take the heat when things go wrong, you will be forced out of your comfort zone at times and you will probably have days when you ask yourself, "self, why did I choose to do this?" But I want you to keep going. Whether you're in a space in life where you're not currently leading anyone at work, in a business, at a non-profit, at home, or otherwise, the principles and pillars in this book are still applicable for when you find yourself in a leadership role in the future. For those leading others, I hope that you found the material in this book to be beneficial, and the action plans are ones that you will start to implement today. I am with you by the way, and will be holding myself accountable to the action plans outlined in every chapter as well.

So, what will you do from here? Where will you be 5 years from now, 10 years, or 20? You have endless potential, and we all only have one shot at creating a legacy in this life. To repeat my statement in the introduction of this book, leadership does not just apply to career and the pursuit of finances. It takes leadership ability to raise children, to mentor people, or any other role where you will be an authority figure. The truth is wherever you are right now in your life, you have what it takes to lead. I'd like to leave you with the list below; each person on this list has either been identified by others as an introvert or has self-identified as one and has changed the world:

Rosa Parks – catalyst behind the Montgomery bus boycott during the civil rights movement

Mark Zuckerberg – creator of Facebook

Shonda Rhimes – creator of the hit television series' Scandal, Grey's Anatomy, How to Get Away With Murder and several others

Elon Musk – CEO and founder of Space X; CEO of Tesla, co-founder of several other companies

Michael Jordan – NBA Hall of Famer, regarded by many as the best basketball player of all time

Barack Obama – 44th president of the United States

Steve Spielberg – world-famous movie director

Issa Rae – creator of the Awkward Black Girl series, and the hit television series Insecure

J.K. Rowlings – creator of the world-renowned Harry Potter series

Warren Buffet – world's most successful stock investor

Bill Gates – founder of Microsoft

Albert Einstein – world famous theoretical physicist

Although the people on this list have accomplished amazing things throughout their lives, they are human, just like you. Despite their fears, they made a choice to take the road less traveled. They made a choice to lead. I wonder how many of you reading this will decide to make that choice. For those that are ready, I am excited for you! It takes time, and none of us are perfect, but every day you can make progress.

In 2014, my wife and I were attending a social justice event at Friendship-West Baptist Church in Dallas. There were around 100 people in the audience at the church. On the stage, there was a panel of 4 middle school and high school students. The moderator would ask the students various questions, and they would respond with their opinions and feelings on the topic. I'll never forget one boy on the panel. The first time the moderator called his name and asked him for input, he held the microphone to his mouth, and with his hand visibly shaking, he didn't say anything. After 10 seconds of silence, the moderator moved on to the next question, which one of the other students on stage jumped in and answered quickly. Another few rounds of questions went by, and the moderator asked the boy a question again. Similar to the first time around, he had the microphone held up, but no words came out. The moderator made a comment to the crowd,

"It's ok, you all know it can be intimidating up here on stage under the lights and all. So, it's ok."

As I sat there in the crowd, I felt a deep sense of connection with that boy on stage. I realize now that it was because when I looked at that boy, I saw myself. I saw myself standing speechless in choir rehearsal that day in 7th grade in front of my choir director. Now I was witnessing a boy around that same age struggling to express himself. When their segment ended, the students got up to exit the stage. Something inside me was telling me to get up from my seat and go talk to the boy when he got off stage. I wanted to encourage him, tell him that he was strong, that he was powerful, that nothing was wrong with him, and that everything would be ok. I wanted to share my story with him in hopes that it would be an inspiration and help him if he ever got down on himself.

Sadly, I ignored that feeling that was pulling at my spirit, and I didn't get up from my seat. I don't know why I didn't, and it pains me to this day. I have thought about that boy for years since that night, wondering where he is and hoping that he is doing well. I bring that story up because my mission for the remainder of my life is that I will not stay seated if there is someone out there that I can help. It has become a part of my life's purpose going forward.

I sincerely hope you have enjoyed reading this book as much as I have enjoyed writing it. For my fellow introverts out there, I leave you with this quote:

"Don't underestimate me because I'm quiet. I know more than I say, think more than I speak, and observe more than you know" – Michaela Chung

ACKNOWLEDGMENTS

The stories, experiences, and principles covered in this book would have been implausible without my life being touched by so many people. I have been a part of several high-performing teams in my professional career that helped to give me the experience necessary to become a leader. I also have had so many people pour into me in my personal life, and they have truly helped to mold me into the man that I am today.

I would like to thank my first manager, Roland Williams, who took a chance and gave me my first engineering job out of college at Lockheed Martin. I'd also like to thank all of my co-workers that worked with and believed in me on the F-16 and F-35 programs. In particular Brian Fields, who took me under his wing and taught me everything that he knew over countless hours before leaving our program. As well as Robbie Vaughn who stood by when I had to give my first big presentation in a packed room as a kid fresh out of school. I would like to thank Jan Killion, the manager of our Engineering Leadership Development Program at Lockheed, for exposing me to several aspects of leadership for the first time.

I'd like to thank my next manager, Aaron Weick, for onboarding me and giving me an opportunity at Bell Helicopter, as well as all of my co-workers that worked on the V-22 program with me during my time there.

Next, Marty Pecarina and Rod Woodson for hiring me into my first true leadership role as a Project Engineer for a program at L3 Technologies in Greenville, Texas. To my mentor Chris Byrd, for his lessons, stories, and guidance that he gave as I worked to navigate my way as a leader for the first time. I'd also like to thank several of the other Project Engineers and Program Managers that worked with and believed in me, including Gary

Garrison, Mike Ford, Mark Ardvison, Shawn Stegall, AJ Avery, Mario Mojica, Paul Brown, Shaun King, Jeff Page, Mark Watts, and Jeff Hostetler. In addition, all of my other co-workers, including but not limited to several engineers, finance, contracts, operations, and supply chain.

Lastly, at my current company, there are so many people to thank, and we continue to make magic happen. At the risk of leaving someone out, I will just say a huge thank you to everyone that I've had the pleasure of working with at Raytheon.

Despite the success that I've seen in my career, none of it means anything without my family and friends. I would like to thank my late grandfather Fred Lee, who has been an inspiration for me my entire life, even though I never met him. My late grandfather Moses Pemberton Sr., for his humor, his wisdom and his character that I miss so dearly. My late grandmother Maude for her warmth, her giving heart, and for how she always believed in me. My late grandmother Mary for her strength, her love, and for taking care of me when I was at some of my lowest points in college. There are so many people in my life that played a role in me being who I am, and where I am today. So at the risk of forgetting or leaving anyone out, I would just like to thank my family, my friends, my godparents, my classmates and everybody that has poured into my life throughout the years. I am forever grateful.

Next, I would like to thank my immediate family.

My sister Valerie for being my friend, my advocate, and the best sister I could have ever asked for. Her husband Marcus, who has become like a brother to me, as well as their children Amia, Uriah and...(a baby girl that is on the way as of this writing!). Love you all.

My mom and dad. To my mom for her outgoing personality, her strength, her belief in me, and her prayers for me throughout the years. To my dad for his calm demeanor, his wisdom, his faith in me and his prayers for me throughout the years. Thank you both for always having my back, and for wanting the best for me. Love you.

To my son, Amari, daddy loves you, and is so proud of the young boy that you are growing into. To my daughter, Aminah, daddy loves you, and is excited to see the young girl that you are becoming. To my wife Octavia, you are my rock and my best friend. I thank you for being by my side through good and bad times, my wins and my losses. I can't imagine going through this life without you, love you.

Finally, I would like to thank my Lord and Savior, Jesus Christ, for being the example of how I hope to live my life. By helping others, valuing others, and living a life of kindness and love. I fall and make mistakes, but I'm so thankful to have your spirit to keep me at peace.

Made in the USA
Columbia, SC
29 December 2021

52979753R00124